SPECTACULAR WINERIES
of Ontario

A CAPTIVATING TOUR OF ESTABLISHED, ESTATE, AND BOUTIQUE WINERIES
Photography by Steven Elphick

Published by

PANACHE
PANACHE PARTNERS

1424 Gables Court
Plano, TX 75075
469.246.6060
Fax: 469.246.6062
www.panache.com

Publishers: Brian G. Carabet and John Shand

Printed in Canada

Distributed by Independent Publishers Group
800.888.4741

PUBLISHER'S DATA

Spectacular Wineries of Ontario

Library of Congress Control Number: 2012930877

ISBN 13: 978-0-9832398-6-4
ISBN 10: 098323986X

First Printing 2012

10 9 8 7 6 5 4 3 2 1

Right: Between the Lines Winery, page 16

Previous Page: 13th Street Winery, page 116

Panache Partners, LLC, is dedicated to the restoration and
conservation of the environment. Our books are manufactured
with strict adherence to an environmental management system in
accordance with ISO 14001 standards, including the use of paper
from mills certified to derive their products from well-managed forests.
We are committed to continued investigation of alternative paper
products and environmentally responsible manufacturing processes
to ensure the preservation of our fragile planet.

SPECTACULAR WINERIES
of Ontario

Inniskillin Wines, page 46

Culture does not exist in a vacuum; it needs context and company to take shape and thrive, and to make others believe in its existence. The culture of Ontario wine expands with each grape harvest; with each festival and new local kitchen, it comes into sharper focus. As Ontario's potential is being transformed into reality, we're right in the middle of it all. What fortune to be part of this meaningful period in winemaking history, and how great to have these trailblazing wineries collected in one magnificent volume.

The rise of Ontario wine matters because wine is an expression of culture, a reflection of people and places, of shared beliefs and attitudes. Ontario has its own unique wine culture, but how did it come to be? Because of its cold climate, Ontario was once thought to be at a disadvantage to its temperate European fine wine counterparts. Yet Ontarian vineyards thrive from the proximity of the Great Lakes—Ontario and Erie—which prove to be repositories of heat in the cooler months, fending off the first frosts of the season and sheltering the landscape from the ravages of the arctic cold.

Willing winemakers with a passion for the industry arrived in the 1860s at Canada's southernmost point of Pelee Island; however, without the accompanying community of winemakers and patrons, fine wine could not thrive. It wasn't until 1975 that Donald Ziraldo and Karl Kaiser founded Inniskillin, Canada's first commercial winery of the post-Prohibition era. Success trickled, then flowed, and it continues to grow, winning over hearts, minds, and palates at home and abroad.

As I travel eastward along the south shore of Lake Ontario, my heart quickens when I catch the first glimpse of the rising Escarpment. I know vineyards will soon appear under its protective embrace, and I marvel at the fortuitous conditions that permit rich fruit to grow. Along the North Shore of Lake Erie, I see the green-gold fields of corn and tobacco that Canadians would have seen 100 years ago. In their stead are upright vines ordered in neat rows.

In Prince Edward County I feel the stinging cold wind swirling off the lake, and I know that its moderating effect will result in another year's supply of riveting wine, as sharp on the tongue as the early spring breeze and as heart-warming and uniquely Canadian as an artist's landscape.

Welcome to Ontario's wine country.

John Szabo
Master Sommelier

Photograph by Christopher Wadsworth

Crown Bench Estates Winery, page 130

INTRODUCTION

Ontario is rich in not only history and culture, but also geography. From a sparsely populated wilderness in the north to Niagara Falls in the south and the bustling metropolis Toronto—ancestral home to many of the Iroquois First Nations—Ontario has developed its own native culture. It also boasts rich soil, a temperate climate, and an idyllic latitude, making the province the perfect growing location for some of the finest cool-climate wines in the world.

Grapes are a native natural resource to Ontario. Canadians have been making wine since the 1800s, yet it has only been since the 1970s that modern winemaking has become a serious industry in Ontario. Despite its relatively young heritage, Ontario is making a name for itself by producing world-renowned wines.

Ontario seems to defy all preconceived notions about growing grapes in cool, inland environs by producing luscious and enticing wines in an array of varietals. Unlike warm-climate grapes that ripen quickly into fruit which produces sweet wines that are low in acidity and high in alcohol, the cool-climate vines of Ontario ripen slowly, accumulating their flavor gently over a longer period of time. As a result, Ontario wines possess a complex and balanced quality which is high in acidity and mineral flavors, making them particularly food-friendly.

Like the diverse history of the province, Ontario wineries are as varied as the vintages they produce. From large-scale facilities with cutting-edge technology to charming family vineyards, you will find adventure and romance in the gently sloping hills and around the sparkling lakes of Ontario's wineries. Along your travels, you will encounter artisans inspired by the winemaking culture of Ontario who specialize in culinary treats, fashionable accessories, and crucial wine storage solutions.

To prepare you for your journey, *Spectacular Wineries of Ontario* will take you on an eye-opening tour of the four distinct Ontario wine regions—Niagara Escarpment and Twenty Valley, Niagara-on-the-Lake, Lake Erie North Shore and Pelee Island, and Prince Edward County. The final chapter, Off the Vine, offers a glimpse into the restaurants, stores, and tasting rooms proud to serve and sell the wines and products related to the winemaking industry. Gorgeous photography and captivating descriptions make this landmark publication a wonderfully comprehensive guide to falling in love with Ontario wine.

Megalomaniac Wines, page 164

Rosehall Run Vineyards, page 238

Founded in 1947, Grape Growers of Ontario provides winemakers and grape growers with the resources to better their industry. Among its responsibilities, Grape Growers of Ontario negotiates minimum prices for all grapes sold to processors. Through the organization's help, Ontario has become the top producer of wine in Canada. Ninety-four percent of the grapes grown in Ontario go to commercial winemaking production. The other six percent go toward the production of other grape-based products: juice, jams, home winemaking supplies, and other foods.

Although Canadians have been growing grapes for the production of wine and other grape-based consumables for centuries, the modern winemaking industry of Ontario benefitted from a 20th-century renaissance of the process. Native to Ontario, the vitis labrusca or "fox grapes," such as Concord and Catawba, are identifiable by their slip-skin and sweet nature. Their sugary and musky flavor is ideal for making juice, jelly, and jam, which was largely the market that Ontario was serving. With a desire to become a diversified source of agricultural products, growers aimed for the booming wine industry, whose standards were set by dry European table wines at the time. In order to become top contenders in the world market, vineyards began to experiment with vitis vinifera, a complex grape of premium quality and the known origin of Europe's beloved table wine. Between 1989 and 1991, 8,000 acres of labrusca and hybrid vines were removed, and over time growers replaced them with vitis vinifera vines. The shift from labrusca to vinifera grapes impacted growers and stimulated the region's 15,000-acre wine industry.

Photograph courtesy of Grape Growers of Ontario

Grape Growers of Ontario strives to expand the markets for Ontario wines both within Canada and internationally. That mission places members of the organization anywhere from within the walls of government facilities as lobbyists for legislation and policies that affect the grape and wine industry to the verdant sloping vineyards of Ontario's varying wineries. The organization serves as an advocate for and an invaluable resource to its members. Funded entirely by grape growers who pay a fee per metric tonne of grapes sold, Grape Growers of Ontario advocates working together to achieve sustainable growth and profitability by creating an improved environment for Ontario grape producers. Vineyard expansions, upgrades, and changes with a focus on vinifera production have helped Ontario gain international attention. Of particular notice is Ontario's icewine, a top competitor in the market and signature vintage for the region.

Grape Growers of Ontario's goal to see that the markets for Ontario grapes and wines expand domestically and internationally has already begun to materialize due to the passionate research, continued innovation, and pioneering spirit the organization's growers apply daily.

Photograph by Denis Cahill

VINTNERS QUALITY ALLIANCE ONTARIO

For years, experts said that growing wine in Ontario simply could not be done; popular opinion claimed that the topography and climate of the second-largest Canadian province was not conducive to healthy, plentiful grape harvests. However, the young wine industry of Ontario stands as proof that not only can grapes be harvested and wine produced there, but Ontario wine can be produced well. The unique terroirs of Ontario—some carved from ancient glacial drifts, others sitting nearly in the middle of cool waterways—yield some of the best cool-climate wines in the world.

The creation of Vintners Quality Alliance (VQA) in 1989 set a global standard for the industry. A wine's quality lies in the soil from which its grapes are grown. Winemakers speak of terroir: the combination of geography, geology, and climate in which wine grapes are grown. The qualities of terroir are best expressed in the interpretation of the grapes from fruit to wine through the processes of care given to the vines, as well as the crush, fermentation, and aging of the grapes. Winemaking lends character to wine but, fundamentally, all wine is an expression of its origin. VQA aids winemakers in this pursuit. With more than 130 wineries in Ontario growing an array of varietals and producing the wine in different styles, VQA's role is significant.

VQA provides the structure and sense of place, defining the winemaking regions of Ontario, setting wine production and labeling standards, and enforcing compliance with those standards. VQA is managed by VQA Ontario, an independent agency which ensures truth in labeling for consumers and maintains a consistent application of regulations for winemakers. The organization serves also to protect Ontario's terms of origin as well as certain wine names, ensuring that the terms are not misused. Each wine is evaluated by VQA Ontario before it is sold to the consumer, passing a taste test, a full chemical analysis, and a label review before hitting the shelves.

Nearly all of Ontario's vineyards stretch across the southern part of the province, taking advantage of the temperate climate, diversity of glacial soils, and the moderating effect of the Great Lakes, to produce mature fruit and complex wines. All VQA wines are made from 100-percent Ontario-grown grapes, the majority of which come from the four primary wine appellations of Ontario. VQA makes distinctions between the appellations based on their physical properties such as soil and underlying geology, temperature, precipitation, and topography.

Winemaking in Ontario is continually evolving. Exceptional wines made in particular appellations continue to emerge and enrich the styles of Ontario wines. The same spirit of innovation that created VQA and nurtured a thriving industry continues with diversity in approach and willingness to experiment. It promises to bring more of the best out of this region.

Huff Estates Winery, page 222

CONTENTS

Stratus Vineyards, page 90

PRINCE EDWARD COUNTY

LAKE ERIE NORTH SHORE AND PELEE ISLAND

EMERGING REGIONS

OFF THE VINE

Colaneri Estate Winery, page 26

PondView Estate Winery, page 66

Strewn, page 96

Vignoble Rancourt Winery, page 106

Between the Lines Winery

Niagara-on-the-Lake

The motto at Between the Lines Winery is "do everything with two heads." Brothers Yannick and Greg Wertsch combined two heads and 10 years of studies in viticulture and winemaking to open their dream winery. Raised in Wurttemberg, Germany, they relocated to a farm in Ontario as teenagers in the late '90s. With help from an investor, the late Jim Forbes, they turned the family farm, which they bought from their parents, into a winery. They were thankful for the property's established vines, which meant they didn't need to start from scratch.

Housed in a charming fire-truck red barn, the winery is aptly named after its location, on Four Mile Creek Road between lines 5 and 6. In its first year, the winery produced an impressive 1,800 cases, a number expanding steadily but carefully. The brothers produce riesling, gewürztraminer, chardonnay, pinot gris, pinot noir, cabernet franc, and merlot, as well as lemberger. Although the vineyard is 45 acres, set up as a rectangle with a north-south orientation, the winery is small and intimate, which allows for a transparent experience where patrons can see everyone involved in the operation.

Greg and Yannick don't utilize a typical winemaking style. They favor what they consider the best way to extract the most flavor, at times blending a new world approach with a traditional style. The riesling is made in the traditional German style, gewürztraminer in the Alsation way, and the cabernet franc in a bold, new world fashion.

Top and Middle: The winery combines old world and new world techniques for the perfect wine.

Bottom: Veraison at Between the Lines, still a couple of weeks until harvest.

Facing Page: The beautifully restored barn houses the production and retail areas, which makes for an intimate experience.
Photographs by Steven Elphick

Niagara-on-the-Lake is known for its cooler-climate approach to winemaking, which delivers very aromatic and fine wines. Seven different types of soil cut across with the rows of vines, allowing for more variety, which is unique and fortunate. The winery's flagship wine is the Lemberger, commonly produced in Central and Eastern Europe.

Yannick and Greg are among the youngest vintners in the area, but the duo does not let their age get in the way of their aspiration to create the finest wine. Greg teaches several courses at a nearby college, everything from wine management to vineyard production. He jokes that he is as young as the students he teaches, but the truth is that his winemaking wisdom far exceeds his years. The brothers have put incredible amounts of research and testing into their winery, which certainly comes across in the quality and taste of the wines they create.

Top: Brothers Yannick and Gregory own and operate Between the Lines.

Middle: The line-up includes the 18-month oak-aged Reserve Series.

Bottom: Between the Lines Winery is open-concept and keeps all its areas accessible to the public.

Facing Page: Morning fog over the 45-acre vineyards, with a wind machine peeking through the dew.
Photographs by Steven Elphick

Riesling
Goes well with seafood or spicy Thai curry.

Lemberger
Great with cigars or served with braised steaks.

Cabernet Franc
Fantastic when paired with venison.

Tastings
Open to the public, year-round

FAMILY
ESTATE WINERY

BETWEEN THE LINES

LONG. -79.10. LAT. 43.19

Cattail Creek Estate Winery

Niagara-on-the-Lake

The great scientist Louis Pasteur once proclaimed, "Chance favors the prepared mind." Such is true for Ken and Renate Dyck, who traded their life savings for 23 acres of land. Situated near Renate's childhood vineyard—run by her father—a plot of existing pear trees was replaced with grapevines, and a small farmhouse was restored before the arrival of first-born child Warren. The family grew the business to100 acres spread over four vineyards between 1971 until the early 1990s. Years of preparation met opportunity when a local winery commissioned the Dycks to plant an experimental block of German riesling on their promising property. The vines planted in 1976 now comprise one of the oldest blocks of riesling in Ontario.

Boasting over 100 acres of varietals, Cattail Creek Estate Winery has four vineyards within Four Mile Creek—a sub-appellation of Niagara-on-the-Lake—where estate-grown fruit transforms into VQA wine. While the estate riesling and chardonnay receive the most international acclaim, a wall of awards devoted to other vintages such as merlot, pinot noir, cabernet franc, and cabernet sauvignon prove that quality runs in the family, right next to success.

Top: The beautiful cattails grow in the creek that meanders through the vineyards of Cattail Creek Estate Winery.

Bottom: One of the oldest blocks of riesling in Ontario, planted in 1976, produces Cattail Creek's Riesling Reserve, a wine with stunning complexity and longevity.

Facing Page: The winery, built in 2006, houses the production facility, tasting bar, and boutique. Inspired by its viticultural roots, the building is nestled in the renowned riesling vineyards.
Photographs by Steven Elphick

Roselyn Dyck, daughter of Ken and Renate, dreamed about owning a winery from the time she could drive. Being raised on a vineyard and surrounded by the culture, her interest in wine led to a bachelor of science and a diploma from the Wine and Spirits Education Trust in London. After nine years of professional experience, and the birth of her son, Alex, Roselyn returned home to concentrate on the brand and development of the family winery.

Warren Dyck, son of Ken and Renate, is also invested in the vineyard, applying his passion for viticulture in the field. Through ongoing research and meticulous experimentation, he and his father lead the vineyard's operation and production.

Dedicated to the earth, the family practices sustainable methods of farming. Constant experimentation of growing techniques and detailed soil management help reduce the use of chemicals and keep vines in prime condition. Along with leaf canopy management, natural elements are maximized in lieu of manmade methods that can disrupt fragile organic life. These practices, along with careful equipment selection, energy efficiency, minimal water use, and recycling, are all applied daily. Additionally, the Dycks are extremely sensitive to the creek behind the winery and its inhabitants. Rainwater collection helps to offset the

Top: A small selection of the winery's awards won to date includes prestigious Cuvee Awards for the 2006 Barrel Fermented Vidal Icewine and 2007 Barrel Fermented Chardonnay.

Bottom: The Cattail Creek Estate Winery family: founders Ken and Renate, vineyard manager Warren, winery manager Roselyn, and grandson Alex.

Facing Page: The wines of Cattail Creek Estate Winery are small lot wines, each handcrafted, hand-bottled, and hand-labeled, reflecting the care and dedication shown from grape growing to winemaking.
Photographs by Steven Elphick

amount of water used, while buffer zones along the creek reduce erosion and encourage wildlife such as ducks, blue herons, and muskrats to inhabit the water and its embankment.

Another creature close to the family's heart is the inspiration behind one of the four collections of Cattail Creek wines. Cat-astrophe wine honors the beloved history of precocious pets—domestics and strays—whose warm features can be found on each label, along with their name. A portion of the proceeds from each bottle sold goes to the Lincoln County Humane Society, ensuring a safe sanctuary for felines that are in-between homes.

Like her husband, Renate spends her days in the vineyards, watching over the grapes or toiling away in the garden and teaching grandson Alex about life's important lessons: nurture the earth which nurtures you, and chance often favors the prepared.

Top: Barrels play an important part in the winemaking at Cattail Creek; each barrel is specially selected to complement the flavors of the wines.

Bottom: Cattail Creek's stunning tasting bar is created from field stones sourced from the very vineyard on which the winery is located.

Facing Page: Sustainable methods help ensure that the land will remain healthy for generations to come.
Photographs by Steven Elphick

Estate Pinot Noir
Pair with fettuccine with wild mushroom and sausage ragù.

Estate Riesling
Pair with slow-roasted pork belly sliders topped with caramelized onions and drizzled with maple syrup.

Vidal Icewine
Pair with cream of cauliflower soup drizzled with truffle oil.

Tastings
Open to the public daily, year-round

Colaneri Estate Winery

St. David's Bench

Passion is the heartbeat of Colaneri Estate Winery. It began with a love story in Frosolone, Italy, between Mike and Nick Colaneri's parents and continued overseas with the love of tradition, family, and wine. Founded by the brothers and their wives, the namesake winery sits on a beautiful stretch of land on St. David's Bench in Niagara-on-the-Lake. The bench was carved out when glaciers formed the Niagara Escarpment, creating a moisture-rich environment perfect for grape growing. It is also stunning topography, where the Niagara River meets Lake Ontario.

After acquiring an existing vineyard on the bench that originally produced French hybrid-style grapes, the Colaneri family replaced and planted new varietals such as pinot grigio, cabernet sauvignon, syrah, gewürztraminer, riesling, cabernet franc, merlot, pinot noir, chardonnay, and vidal.

The c-shaped, 31,000-square-foot winery honors the family name and features a taste of Italy. The family designed it in a Romanesque style, reminiscent of the streets of Tuscany. Nestled among the 25 acres of vineyards, it rises amid the vines like a coliseum, majestic and timeless. Floor-to-ceiling arched windows bathe the interior with light and allow for stunning views of the property. From the retail store, patrons can see the production area and all of its exciting processes. The outdoor patio offers visitors a bucolic way to savor their wine, enjoying a view of the vineyard below with Toronto visible on the horizon on clear days.

Top: Passion begins at the grand entrance that welcomes visitors from all over the world.
Photograph courtesy of Colaneri Estate Winery

Bottom: The winery, with its bell tower, brings a taste of Romanesque style to Ontario.
Photograph courtesy of Colaneri Estate Winery

Facing Page: The winery's tasting room and retail store is where wines can be savored and enjoyed among the family memorabilia.
Photograph by Steven Elphick

Colaneri Estate Winery is a tribute to heritage and the traditions the family holds dear. In fact, each varietal was selected by a family member and corresponding labels were made to represent a distinctive attribute or trait about that person. The wine labels are etched in the style of Leonardo da Vinci, each telling an aspect of the family story.

Above: The winery nods to Italian style.
Photograph courtesy of Colaneri Estate Winery

Right: Colaneri uses only the best natural cork to beautifully age its wines.
Photograph by Steven Elphick

Facing Page: Each family member is holding the bottles designed for them. Michael, Liberina "Betty," Mike, Tara, Christopher, Nicholas, and Nick Colaneri.
Photograph by Steven Elphick

With Italian names adorning the labels, guests and wine enthusiasts enjoy the wine and get to know the family as each label is unveiled. Cavallone depicts the horse that is majestic and a free spirit, while Coraggioso, the courageous and bold bull, protects the family. Visione represents the eagle that soars above with the vision of what is to be, and Mistera expresses the intrigue and suspense of what lies behind the mask of mystery. Stellucha is the little star that glides across the floor dancing amid the stars, and Unita symbolizes the united family gathered and enjoying a meal lovingly prepared. Pensiere means deep in thought and depicts the wine's complexity with architectural tones. Virtuoso, another wine, signifies the talent to entertain in the midst of those seeking to be enlightened. Insieme was so named in honor of Maria and Joseph Colaneri, who did everything together. And last but not least, Paese remembers Frosolone, Italy, where it all began with the Colaneris.

Above: As individual as the varietals they contain, each label caresses the bottle to reveal the story.
Photograph by Steven Elphick

Facing Page Top: The winery is illuminated, majestic and timeless, as it adorns the night sky.
Photograph courtesy of Colaneri Estate Winery

Facing Page Bottom: The wine lies in wait, aging to perfection in the barrel cellar.
Photograph by Steven Elphick

Colaneri's wines are produced using the appassimento technique, which is a natural way to extract water from the grapes to intensify the flavors and aromas. Through dedication and perseverance, the Colaneri family insists on hand picking only the best grapes to make premium wines that meet the standards of the Vintners Quality Alliance. Choosing quality rather than quantity gives way to the full-bodied results of appassimento, ripasso—a re-fermentation process that adds flavor and body to the wine—and recioto, any wine made from grapes dried to bring out the sweetness. Every wine tasting conveys the family's love of tradition, pride, and passion, leaving visitors with an unforgettable experience.

Above Left: Only hand-picked grapes, prepared in the appassimento style, are used for Colaneri wine.
Photograph by Steven Elphick

Above Right: Colaneri's time-tested techniques provide a more intensely aromatic and flavored wine.
Photograph by Steven Elphick

Left: Only the best equipment is used for the winery's mission of quality over quantity.
Photograph courtesy of Colaneri Estate Winery

Facing Page: The winery is surrounded by the vines.

Cavallone Pinot Grigio
Delicious with pasta primavera, alia e olio, and frittata.

Coraggioso Cabernet Sauvignon
The perfect mate for red meats.

Visione Syrah
Ideal with venison, pepper steak, and salsiccia.

Mistera Gewürztraminer
Incredible with turkey, ham, risotto, or Thai food.

Tastings
Open to the public daily, year-round

COLANERI
ESTATE WINERY

Diamond Estates

Niagara-on-the-Lake

Located in scenic Niagara-on-the-Lake, Diamond Estates is bringing green practices and global reach to the Niagara Peninsula. Behind the doors of their state-of-the-art winemaking facility, Murray Marshall, president and CEO, Tom Green, vice president of winemaking and operations, and winemakers Jason Roller and Scott McGregor collaborate both creatively and strategically to turn out nationally recognized wines worthy of the region's rich reputation. Thanks to the estate's deep bonds with 25 different grape growing partners throughout the region, the Diamond Estates team has the supply and latitude to produce a broad range of some of the most accessible and palate-friendly wines in the business.

Diamond Estates, which sits on 30 acres, is home to a host of labels including 20 Bees, Dan Aykroyd, FRESH, Lakeview Cellars, EastDell, and NHL Alumni Wines Hat Trick and operates Diamond Estates The Wine Store in Toronto's Cliffside Plaza.

Given the region's ideal conditions, it's no wonder that Diamond Estates is able to produce some of Ontario's more popular red, white, rosé, sparkling, icewine, and dessert wines. Its selections open with the fresh and unassuming 20 Bees table wines. Inspired by the label's early growers and original winemaker, 20 Bees wines provide a fun and accessible portal into everyday wine appreciation. Likewise, the celebrity-branded Dan Aykroyd wines have been crafted in collaboration with the actor to mirror his own personality. The result is an affable, everyman's collection of table wines, icewines, and collectors' wines structured around Dan's personal tastes.

Top: The core team at Diamond Estates includes Tom Green, Murray Marshall, Scott McGregor, and Jason Roller.

Bottom: The winery's barrel cellar is outfitted with state-of-the-art stainless steel tanks.

Facing Page: The grapevines gently warm as the sun begins to rise.
Photographs by Steven Elphick

Diamond Estates' Lakeview Cellars label caters to the high-end reserve market and tips its hat to the original Lakeview Cellars property, which overlooked Lake Ontario in Beamsville. The Lakeview Cellars brand contains an extensive icewine selection that includes cabernet sauvignon, cabernet franc, riesling, and gewürztraminer and is known for producing single varietal wines from the best vintages.

Combine the favorite national pastime with winemaking and philanthropy and you get the formula for the estate's NHL Alumni Wines Hat Trick, a series of blends that raises a glass to the rich history of Canadian hockey. Each light, fruit-forward wine in the series is the result of collaboration between former NHL stars and Diamond Estates' winemakers. Fifty cents from every bottle of Hat Trick sold goes to the NHL Alumni Association to support charitable causes and promote the game of hockey. Diamond Estates has also partnered with Mothers Against Drunk Driving to create and package an entire line of non-alcoholic wines for designated drivers and teetotalers.

At the front of the estate, Diamond's modest tasting cabin is open daily, year-round and features selections from even more of Diamond Estate's labels, including the easy-drinking and affordable 20 Bees, EastDell Estate blends, and FRESH wines, which feature the fun, unconventional varietal blends of gewürztraminer/ riesling, sauvignon blanc/chardonnay, cabernet/gamay, and merlot/syrah. And thanks to a solid eco-objective, the vines aren't the only green thing on the estate. Sustainable winemaking practices contribute greatly to Diamond Estates' ethos and identity. Winemaking waste water is filtered with an energy efficient Biobed purification system and recycled for use in the estate's grey-water systems, rainwater is diverted from the roof into the gardens, and the production areas stay clean thanks to a low-water line cleaning system that reduces water usage by 50 percent during harvest season. The planned installation of 36,000 square feet of solar panels on the roof is the icing on Diamond Estates' eco-friendly cake.

Right: 2010 Reserve wines will rest and age in their stacked barrels for two to three years before being released.

Facing Page Top: The winery's bottling line sanitizes and fills each bottle.

Facing Page Bottom: Three 25-ton pneumatic bladder presses squeeze luscious juices free from the grapes.
Photographs by Steven Elphick

Growth continues at Diamond Estates, where a state-of-the-art retail and hospitality building is in development at the company's Niagara-on-the-Lake location. The new digs will house all of the same brands that Diamond Estates owns today, plus any new ones that come down through the pipeline in years to come. Diamond Estates also represents international brands galore: Vina San Pedro and Emiliana from Chile; Andre and Francois Lurton, Fat Bastard, and Rodet from France; Anciano from Spain; Long Flat, Kilikanoon, and Angus the Bull from Australia—an impressive global lineup with a solid Canadian foundation.

Above: A variety of labels are produced at the winery's state-of-the-art production facility.

Left and Facing Page: Climate-controlled, low-light tanks ensure optimum quality control.
Photographs by Steven Elphick

EastDell Black Cab
Delicious with grilled double-cut pork chops stuffed with goat cheese and dried cranberries and seasoned with cracked black pepper.

Hat Trick Red
Pair with hockey night favorites like barbecue black peppercorn steaks, Italian sausages, or meat pizza.

Dan Aykroyd Merlot
A perfect match for a juicy T-bone served with asparagus and roasted red peppers, pork tenderloin served with tart cranberry sauce, or gourmet pizza topped with duck confit.

20 Bees Pinot Grigio
Serve with fresh oysters on the half shell, freshly squeezed lemon, and medium-spiced red pepper jelly.

Tastings
Open daily, year-round

THE WINERY

Hinterbrook Estate Winery

Niagara-on-the-Lake

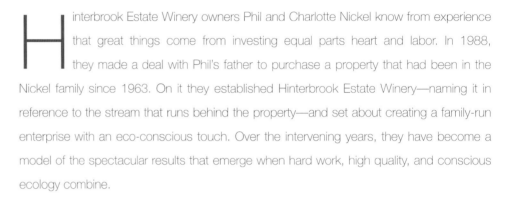

Hinterbrook Estate Winery owners Phil and Charlotte Nickel know from experience that great things come from investing equal parts heart and labor. In 1988, they made a deal with Phil's father to purchase a property that had been in the Nickel family since 1963. On it they established Hinterbrook Estate Winery—naming it in reference to the stream that runs behind the property—and set about creating a family-run enterprise with an eco-conscious touch. Over the intervening years, they have become a model of the spectacular results that emerge when hard work, high quality, and conscious ecology combine.

With an eye to someday establishing his own winery, Phil spent the early years planting, tending, and perfecting his vines, developing a superior vineyard and supplying top-quality grapes to a large area winery. In the meantime, Phil dreamed of making his own select wines from those same grapes he had taken such care in establishing. He strategically planted a selection of varietals so that when the time was right he'd be ready with mature vines.

Over a period of time in 2009, the family met around the dinner table and made the decision to take the winemaking plunge. They would establish Hinterbrook using the latest winemaking technologies and produce premium wines with an earth-friendly approach. Each family member brought a special skill; from among the core group, the Nickels had the winery's administration, marketing, and winemaking aspects covered. With such a solid foundation, starting a family business seemed not only natural, but feasible.

Top: Hinterbrook's entrance sign is styled after its bottle label.

Bottom: Merlot leaves in the fall.

Facing Page: Riesling vines backed by the brilliant fall colors of a neighboring woodlot.
Photographs by Steven Elphick

With that commitment to technology and ecology in place, the Nickels hung out their shingle, setting up shop in an onsite production facility and tasting room—a building that was functional at best—and began designing what would become their dream winery.

Today the clean, crisp, and contemporary buildings stand as physical representations of the Nickels' commitment to modern winemaking technology. The facility utilizes systems for geothermal heating and cooling, rainwater collection, and low-chemical sanitation. A 1,000-square-foot solar panel tracks the position of the sun throughout the day and generates enough power during the year to meet the winery's electricity demands.

Producing wine with a minimal environmental impact is no small task. Hinterbrook's contracted winemaking team of Vines To Vintages, led by Natalie Spytkowsky and Darryl Fields, makes every effort to create all of Hinterbrook's varieties—from its Deeply Red, a blend of cabernet franc and cabernet sauvignon, to the specialty franc blanc—in accordance with the Nickels' ethics.

Located in the Niagara Lakeshore sub-appellation, Hinterbrook's vineyards lie close to Lake Ontario, which stands as a constant reminder of the importance of nurturing nature. The lake's moderating breezes in the summer and hot water bottle-effect in the fall increase

Above: Merlot vines cast shadows on the winery building at the end of the day.

Right: Gleaming tanks are ready for another fabulous vintage.

Facing Page Top: Hinterbrook's 10kw solar generator tracks the last rays of the setting sun.

Facing Page Bottom: Three generations of the Nickel family enjoy running the winery operation.
Photographs by Steven Elphick

the grapes' hang time and allow the fruit to gain precious maturity. This extended growing season makes for full-bodied cabernet sauvignons. Likewise, the area's clay base, sandy, loamy topsoil, and significant levels of gravel and rock produce surprising levels of minerality in Hinterbrook's riesling and pinot grigio.

The Nickels' labors have resulted in widespread popularity. To keep up with their more ardent collectors, they have established the Hinterbrook Insider program. Members receive six bottles of wine delivered to their home every three months, a complimentary bottle of icewine, tasting and production notes from the winemaker, recipes, intimate winery tours led by Phil, exclusive wines not available to the retail market, and an invitation to a private After Harvest dinner with winemaker Natalie Spytkowsky, Phil, and Charlotte. It's an earthy, family-style affair, a perfect mirror of Hinterbrook's modest-yet-successful, earth-based business.

Top: An array of impressive wines awaits tasting room visitors.

Bottom: Two of Hinterbrook's many awards won in its first vintage year.

Facing Page: A treasure of aging wines are resting in the barrel room.
Photographs by Steven Elphick

Pinot Noir
Pair with wild mushroom tortellini.

Cabernet Franc Reserve
Pair with grilled black pepper-crusted beef tenderloin.

Sauvignon Blanc
Pair with lobster risotto.

Riesling
Pair with baked ham and potato salad.

Tastings
Open daily in the summer, weekends in the winter

HINTERBROOK
WINERY

Inniskillin Wines

Niagara-on-the-Lake

The piazza's walk at Inniskillin Wines is inset with milestones, marking significant victories and telling the story of one of Ontario's most influential wineries. The engravings reflect stages of growth and the post-Prohibition development of Inniskillin, which has been paramount to the industry. When co-founders Donald Ziraldo and Karl Kaiser entered into the Canadian wine industry in 1975, they received the first winery license since 1929. Neither Donald or Karl could have predicted the pivotal role that Inniskillin would play in revolutionizing the face of Canadian wine and eventually earning respect in the international circuit.

Donald, who was running his family's nursery, and Karl, who had emigrated from Austria in the late '60s, teamed up, committed to the goal of producing premium wines from premium grapes grown in the Niagara Peninsula in an underdeveloped market. As a foreigner, Karl was not impressed with Canadian wines when he first arrived, noticing the foxy flavor that labrusca, or native Canadian grapes, were famous for. Because of his telling palate, Karl was introduced to hybrid and vinifera grapes by Donald, and by 1977 his plantings of chardonnay, riesling, and gamay changed the destiny of Ontario wines forever.

Named after the Inniskilling Fusiliers—an Irish regiment involved in Niagara in the early 1800s—the original Inniskillin Winery was a fruit-packing shed located at Donald's family business, Ziraldo Nursery, just two kilometers south of the existing winery. Built in 1978, the current winery is situated on the Brae Burn farm and is said to resemble the Mondavi Winery in California with its white stucco exterior and romantic archways. The piazza leads guests to the founders' hall, complete with a demonstration kitchen, and to the wine boutique inside of the historic Brae Burn Barn, circa 1920. The onsite vineyard offers panoramic views of

Top: An underground library holds Inniskillin's older vintages, including a vast collection of icewines from the 1980s, such as the legendary 1989 icewine that won the Grand Prix d'Honneur at Vinexpo, Bordeaux.

Bottom: The natural barn beams highlight the vaulted ceiling in the historic Brae Burn Barn retail boutique.

Facing Page: Dramatic renovations to the Brae Burn Barn include a welcoming arched doorway, inspired by the work of famed architect Frank Lloyd Wright.
Photographs by Steven Elphick

the Niagara Peninsula and estate vidal, pinot noir, and shiraz vines. The estate's Montague vineyard is located further inland and is largely responsible for chardonnay, riesling, pinot gris, cabernet franc, and merlot varietals.

Instrumental in forming Canada's appellation of origin system, or Vintners Quality Alliance, Donald was the VQA's founding chairman and assisted in the industry's transition through challenging Free Trade Agreement issues with the U.S. He also led key initiatives for industry growth, including winery tourism strategies, the preservation of agricultural lands, and winery education programs, along with major research efforts at local universities. Meanwhile Karl's extensive knowledge about wine and winemaking garnered him involvement with the Canadian Standards Board and the VQA.

A major turning point for the winery came in 1991, when Karl's 1989 Vidal Icewine won the Grand Prix d'Honneur at Vin Expo Bordeaux, which put Ontario in the international eye. His win was critical for Canada and Inniskillin, the benefits of which influence the region today. Increasing recognition has followed and confirms the winery's renowned reputation, like being deeming the New World Winery of the Year by *Wine Enthusiast* magazine. After a number of mergers, Inniskillin became part of Constellation Brands through the purchase of Vincor International. While Karl retired, Donald went on to lead the

Top: Surrounded by a flock of Canadian geese, the iconic water tower is a symbol of the past.

Bottom: The netted vidal icewine grapes prepare for the first stages of extreme winter exposure.

Facing Page Top: Featuring tasting bars that overlook the vineyards and the Niagara Escarpment, the retail boutique is a highlight for guests, especially when sampling an assortment of icewine styles and vintages, prepared at an exclusive bar.

Facing Page Bottom: The barrel cellar is located underground, offering private and structured tastings among French oak barrels.
Photographs by Steven Elphick

Vineland Research and Innovation Center, and the winery went under new management, leading to the arrival of a new winemaker, Bruce Nicholson.

Hailing from Jackson-Triggs in the Okanagan, Bruce brought with him the expertise and international reputation that Inniskillin required for its next spurt of growth. Continuing with the spirit of innovation innate to the estate, Bruce immediately initiated the recycling of grape pomace for bio-energy. Additionally, since his inclusion to the Inniskillin brand, the brand has received attention from *Drinks International* for making one of the 50 most admired wines in the world. In 2009, he captured the prestigious Premio Speciale Gran from Vinitaly for his Sparkling Vidal Icewine and Oak Aged Vidal Icewine, keeping Inniskillin's reputation and hard work ahead of the curve worldwide. In 73 countries and on 28 airlines, consumers can experience one of Canada's natural treasures.

Above: A hospitality area in the founders' hall profiles a demonstration kitchen and the Riedel Room, often used for entertaining.

Left: Innovative winemaker Bruce Nicholson shows off the source of his environmental initiative: grape pomace used for bio-energy.

Facing Page: The piazza sits adjacent to the founders' hall and provides the perfect setting for eats from the market grill coupled with outdoor tastings.
Photographs by Steven Elphick

Vidal Icewine
Pair with seared scallops in beurre blanc vidal or seafood pasta.

Three Vineyards Cabernet Franc
Pair with tagliatelle beef short ribs, honey mushrooms, and candied garlic or Devil's Rock blue cheese.

Two Vineyards Riesling
Pair with sweet pea panna cotta or heirloom carrot soup.

Montague Vineyard Chardonnay
Pair with hand-cut fries and Upper Canada halloumi cheese with foie gras gravy.

Tastings
Open to the public daily, year-round

Jackson-Triggs
Niagara Estate

One of the country's most awarded wineries, Jackson-Triggs Niagara Estate has acquired over 3,000 merits since 1993 in both domestic and international wine competitions, including a seven-time title of Best Canadian Producer at the International Wine & Spirits Competition in England. Known for two exceptional series of wines—Gold and Silver—the brand offers red, white, sparkling, and icewine varieties for an array of palates and discerning consumers. Currently under the care of master craftsman Marco Piccoli, the wines at Jackson-Triggs Niagara Estate continue to evolve, expand, and exceed industry standards for quality and value, just as they did two decades ago.

Wine aficionados and friends Allan Jackson and Donald Triggs shared a passion for wine and a relentless energy in pursuing the initial buyout of Labatt's Canadian wine interests in 1989. Four years later, Allan and Don created a new company which launched a brand of premium varietal wines that fully expressed the terroir of the region. Through a series of strategic acquisitions and mergers, Vincor International became the largest wine producer in Canada. Both Don and Allan maintained an unwavering commitment to the Canadian wine industry, which has become a statement of their extraordinary business acumen and passion. Don left the company in 2006, when Constellation Brands purchased Vincor International, and Allan followed three years later. They both maintain an active presence in the world of VQA wine.

Top: After a wine is uncorked, the formerly sealed-in aromas and flavors are freed and followed by a tasting adventure.

Middle: The underground barrel cellar is ideal for private tastings and fine dining among French oak barrels. Its dramatic appeal heightens the sensorial experience.

Bottom: As a dedicated winemaker, Marco Piccoli ensures his wine authentically reflects Niagara's terroir.

Facing Page: The state-of-the-art winery is bordered by an herb and vegetable garden for the chef's culinary creations.
Photographs by Steven Elphick

An attractive leverage of their early success, a state-of-the-art winemaking facility was constructed in Niagara-on-the-Lake in 2001. Worthy of the brand they had diligently developed, the simple barn-like design accentuates southern Ontario's geographic personality and terroir. The architecturally ambitious project unites contemporary winemaking technologies with a design response authentic to the region; hospitality and production operations merge seamlessly. The winery can accommodate impressive functions ranging from a summertime concert series in the outdoor amphitheatre to wine events and corporate entertaining throughout the estate.

Situated within the Niagara Peninsula—which is likened to Burgundy, Oregon, and New Zealand for its cool climate—the estate winery produces sauvignon blanc, merlot, cabernet sauvignon, cabernet franc, riesling, pinot noir, chardonnay, and icewine rivaling those found in world-class regions, while reflecting the Niagara region's distinct terroir.

Left: Designed by Toronto-based architects KPMB—Kuwabara, Payne, McKenna, Blumberg—the great hall divides winery production from the retail store and tasting gallery.

Facing Page Top: The tasting gallery hosts flight samplings and culinary experiences while overlooking an adjacent vineyard.

Facing Page Bottom Left: Local cheese and charcuterie boards expose visitors to Niagara's bountiful fare.

Facing Page Bottom Right: Entourage Sparkling, Gold Series, and Silver Series wines are available in a number of varietals from single vineyards.
Photographs by Steven Elphick

Grapes flourish around Niagara-on-the-Lake, thanks to rich, fertile soils and unique microclimates, providing ideal conditions for producing grapes with more complexity and intense flavors than those grown in warmer climates.

Icewine, such as the Gold Series Gewürztraminer, is known for grapefruit aromas with hints of spices. It is an estate specialty along with sparkling wines like Entourage Sparkling Sauvignon Blanc, a bubbly blend of herbaceous and toasty citrus notes. Both selections, like many others, are popular favorites of liquid goodness, delivered from the highly decorated Canadian brand.

Top and Bottom: The chardonnay vineyards are covered in early-morning frost after a fall harvest. As the sun rises the frost thaws and their golden leaves become vibrant.

Facing Page: Fermentation tanks in the atrium benefit from the best views at the winery.
Photographs by Steven Elphick

Entourage Sparkling Merlot
Pair with whipped Brie cheese and merlot-poached cherries.

Silver Series Gewürztraminer
Pair with glass noodle salad with edamame, coriander, and chilies in black sesame vinaigrette.

Silver Reserve Sauvignon Blanc
Pair with golden beet soup with chive crème fraîche.

Delaine Vineyard Syrah
Pair with a cocoa-dusted ribeye with pearl barley risotto.

Tastings
Open to the public daily, year-round

Palatine Hills
Estate Winery

Niagara-on-the-Lake

I n 1972, when John Neufeld purchased the 115-acre property that would become Palatine Hills Estate Winery, running his own viticulture enterprise was the farthest thing from his mind. The farm was rich with cherry, apple, and pear trees, as well as a wealth of labrusca grape varieties which he sold to local winemakers for their sweet table wines. The operation kept the Neufelds busy for close to two decades. In fact, it wasn't until the late '90s that John got the idea to make his own wine. Working with a local vintner, he created his first, an icewine. The wine was a hit, drawing rave reviews and wine-of-the-year awards. It was on the crest of that success that a winemaking friend gave John a piece of advice: you have to either be a grower or a winemaker; you can't do both.

Never one to be told what to do, especially when it comes to his livelihood, John followed his heart instead. So in 2003, against his friend's advice, John decided to wear both the farmer's and the vintner's hats. The rest, as they say, is history.

Ridding the estate of the fruit trees was momentous, but the process proved even more noteworthy than John and Barbara had expected. As they turned over the fields to make way for the grapevines, John discovered musket balls and wartime artifacts. A little research showed that the estate had been a skirmish site in the War of 1812. In honor of the land's rich history, John developed two commemorative wines: an 1812 chardonnay and an 1812 cabernet-merlot, both released for the 2012 bicentennial.

Top, Bottom, and Facing Page: Palatine Hills began producing its own wine in the late 1990s.
Photographs by Steven Elphick

Located near picturesque Niagara-on-the-Lake, Palatine Hills sits at the same latitude as Northern California and shares many of the same grape growing advantages. Both enjoy a moderate climate and benefit from adequate sunshine, but Palatine Hills enjoys a combination of advantages that Northern California does not: a wealth of sandy, sedimentary, clay-like soil, and an inundation of fieldstones.

Those stone and soil conditions have contributed to some significant success. Palatine Hills has racked up more than 20 awards since 2003, including a gold medal at the 2003 Ontario Wine Awards, Ontario Wine of the Year, and a silver medal at the 2007 Canadian Wine Awards.

The area of Palatine Hills itself is not short on advantages. It's far enough away from Toronto to bask in unsurpassed natural beauty yet close enough to benefit from big-city culture. Niagara Falls is a mere 15 miles down the road, and the nearby village of Niagara-on-the-Lake, with its wide Main Street and historic buildings, is a destination spot in itself.

Top: Guests can learn about the region and its history as well as the winery.

Middle and Facing Page: Visitors may sample Palatine Hills wine and then buy their favorites.

Bottom: The wines are produced using state-of-the-art technology.
Photographs by Steven Elphick

These days, the estate is a mighty facility with rotary fermenters, custom pressing, and the latest technology. The Neufelds grow 14 varieties of grapes and produce three tiers of wines: a selection of premier vintages, a range of modest table wines, and a series of unfussy house wines, all overseen by head winemaker Jeff Innes, whose unique ability to understand each wine's capabilities makes him an indispensable member of the team.

A strong team is necessary when you're dealing in such vast quantities. The volume of grapes John grows necessitates that the bulk of the crop be harvested by machine, and where many of their competitors spend their money investing in oak barrels, John is in the process of bringing in an oxygenator that, when combined with oak staves, promises to duplicate the barrel aging experience in a 22,500-gallon tank.

On the estate, visitors gather in the Palatine tasting room. Originally built as a farm-equipment storage shed, the building has 16-foot ceilings and painted floors, giving it the feeling that it was just swept out and opened for business. The welcoming ambience fostered by John and Barbara is undeniable. And it's that grounded, everyman approach to tasting that is sure to earn them their own place of honor in the region's history.

Above and Facing Page: Founder John Neufeld ensures quality wines and a pleasurable guest experience.
Photographs by Steven Elphick

Vineyard Chardonnay
Pairs beautifully with fish, seafood, and truffle-based risotto.

Cabernet Sauvignon
Delicious with gourmet burgers, steak, lamb, and blue cheeses.

Merlot
Outstanding alongside garlic-rosemary crusted lamb.

Vidal Icewine
Delightful with creamy desserts, custards, and pound cake.

Tastings
Open to the public daily, year-round

PALATINE HILLS

Peller Estates

Niagara-on-the-Lake

When Andrew Peller emigrated from Hungary to British Columbia in the 1920s, he looked forward to the opportunities that awaited him, but he also yearned for a taste of Europe. Believing that he could bring wines to Canada in the tradition of his native homeland, Andrew established Andrés Wines in 1964. Today the company is run by Andrew's grandson, John—the third Peller generation to take up winemaking. Over the course of the 20th century, the company migrated from British Columbia to Ontario, becoming one of the most recognizable wineries in Canada.

Named for the company's founder, Peller Estates occupies a French-inspired château amid 25 acres of estate vineyards. With tours offered daily and a wide diversity of events annually, Peller Estates enjoys presenting visitors with its array of varietals. Its various icewines make it an enological wonder. From cabernet franc and vidal icewines to the ice cuvée and ice cuvée rosé—sparkling wine with a dosage of icewine—Peller Estates is an influential presence in the Ontario cool-climate wine industry. As if to illustrate the point, the winery was named Best Canadian Wine Producer of the Year in 2006 and won the Warren Winiarski Trophy for best cabernet sauvignon at the International Wine and Spirit Competition in 2010. Thanks to the talents of estate manager Mark Torrance and executive chef Jason Parsons, guests may sample award-winning wines alongside gourmet fare. Lunch and dinner are served daily, and tastings are available year-round.

Top: Peller Estates icewines.

Middle: The Peller Estates Winery Restaurant is known as a must-do dining experience, rated Extraordinary to Perfection by Zagat.

Bottom: John Peller ensures his grandfather's legacy continues in the wines produced today.

Facing Page: The main building at Peller Estates.
Photographs by Steven Elphick

PondView Estate Winery

Niagara-on-the-Lake

When Giuseppe Puglisi emigrated from Italy to Canada in 1965, he came with an inherent passion for grape growing and winemaking. Guided by generations of experience, Giuseppe passed on years of family trade secrets and tradition to his son Luciano, who is the proprietor of PondView Estate Winery. For decades, Luciano was perfectly content producing the finest grapes, even capturing the coveted Grape King title in 2008/2009, until he attended one of the Okanagan Wine Festivals. There he became inspired to open a boutique winery, embracing the family art form and philosophy that "great wine is a harmony of earth and vine." Supported by his wife Adriana, Luciano established the winery in 2009 and opened its doors in 2010.

Situated within the Four Mile Creek sub-appellation of the Niagara Peninsula, the vineyard is part of Ontario's ever-expanding wine country, with the famous Niagara Falls just minutes away. Here, 60 acres of chardonnay, gewürztraminer, pinot gris, viognier, vidal, and riesling are cultivated to make white wine, icewine, and dessert wine, while cabernet franc, cabernet sauvignon, merlot, pinot noir, and malbec flourish to become red wine and icewine. The varietals thrive in what is largely considered to be the most productive sub-appellation in the Niagara Peninsula. Red shale, high silt, clay loam, and glacial sediments combine to create a nutrient-rich foundation for the plants. In addition, flat plains ensure maximum sunlight exposure while neighboring creeks guarantee optimal soil drainage.

Top: Cabernet sauvignon grapes.

Bottom: PondView Estate Winery at sunset.

Facing Page: Gewürztraminer grapes in the fall.
Photographs by Steven Elphick

Although the area is largely preconceived to be best suited for icewines, cabernet franc surprisingly steals the spotlight at PondView. Praised for an intense combination of black cherry, blackberry, clove, licorice, and vanilla flavors, the smoke-laced and full-bodied wine is effectively alluring to fans of bold reds. As the estate's signature wine—and Luciano's favorite—it accounts for many of the 20-plus awards that the estate received in its first two years. Coming in a close second and boasting notes of toasted nuts, green apples, lemon, and grapefruit, the chardonnay is a dry and fruity white wine with a refreshingly light finish. Other bestsellers include vidal late harvest and vidal icewine, both of which are fruit-filled fantasies containing tones of apricot, peach, pear, mango, and melon.

Top: PondView's signature dark chocolate icewine shooters are decadent.

Bottom: 2010 cabernet franc aging in French oak barrels.

Facing Page Top: PondView Estate Winery at dusk.

Facing Page Bottom: The wine boutique and tasting bar.
Photographs by Steven Elphick

The boutique winery produces approximately 8,000 cases of wine annually. With the help of retail manager Paula Puglisi Aitken—Luciano's sister—and marketing manager Joseph Barbera—Luciano's brother-in-law—Luciano and Adriana organize estate activities, social gatherings, and private tastings each month. Some of the gatherings are exclusive to the wine club. Each club member benefits from wine shipments that alternate monthly and feature proprietor-selected wines, insider secrets, upcoming release dates, messages from the proprietor, and tasting discounts. Higher tiered memberships even receive VIP invites to upcoming events like winemaker dinners, where Luciano personally attends and presents the pairings.

The area's flat topography allows for uninterrupted views of the surrounding countryside. An open-air terrace is the perfect spot to enjoy the sights over an antipasto or cheese platter, while the tasting bar indoors presents inquisitive visitors with a selection of estate-grown, acclaimed vintages such as chardonnay, riesling, pinot grigio, and cabernet franc.

Above Left: The winery is a labor of love for proprietors Luciano and Adriana Puglisi.

Above Right: PondView Estate Winery's wines are award-winning.

Facing Page: Cabernet franc vines in early September.
Photographs by Steven Elphick

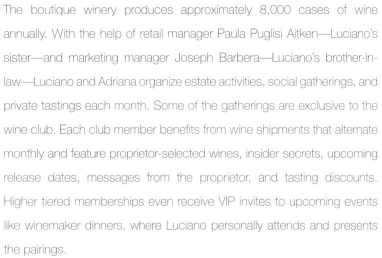

Cabernet Franc
Pair with a braised rack of lamb or beef tenderloin.

Cabernet Franc Icewine
Pair with blue cheese or melted Brie.

Gewürztraminer
Pair with spicy Thai or Indian food.

Tastings
Open to the public daily, year-round

Reif Estate Winery

Niagara-on-the-Lake

The Reif tradition of winemaking began in 1636 in Germany's Rheinphalz region, where 12 generations of family ardently maintained the land in a winemaker's paradise. Seduced by the budding reputation of an emerging viticultural area, Ewald Reif— 11th-generation winemaker—journeyed across continents to survey Niagara and eventually purchased land in 1977. Of immediate priority was uprooting existing vines and replacing them with premium vinifera varietals such as riesling, chardonnay, and cabernet sauvignon. By planting the finest vitis vinifera varietals alongside French hybrids, Ewald became a pioneer in the Niagara wine industry. Over time he expanded the vineyard into a 125-acre farm and in 1982 he opened a winery and boutique, both originally housed in the estate's 1870s coach house.

Klaus W. Reif, like his Uncle Ewald, acquired a deep affection for the region's elevated topography and untouched terroir during a visit to Canada. Upon his return home to Germany, he enrolled in a winemaking program with the intention of eventually returning to Ontario. In 1987, after graduating from the esteemed Geisenheim Institute in Germany with degrees in both enology and viticulture, he was well equipped to take over the reins of the winery as president and enologist. His philosophy that great wines start in the vineyard is the cornerstone of the quality and integrity behind the Niagara River-sourced, estate-bottled wines. Under his leadership, Reif Estate Winery became a pioneer in producing world-class icewines. He also aided in the development of Vintners Quality Alliance as a founding member and partnered in the advancement of the Environmental Charter for Sustainable Winemaking in Ontario.

Top: Vidal icewine grapes are netted for protection from hungry birds until they're ready to be picked at temperatures of -10° C to -12° C.
Photograph by Steven Elphick

Middle: German oak barrels from the original Reif Estate Winery in Nuestadt, Germany, were transported to Canada by sea in 1982.
Photograph courtesy of Reif Estate Winery

Bottom: Klaus W. Reif shares a smile while pondering the more than 400 awards received at both national and international wine competitions in the last 30 years.
Photograph by Steven Elphick

Facing Page: The Reif family crest adorns the doors of the new wine boutique, constructed in 2008.
Photograph by Steven Elphick

In 1990, Klaus was joined by Roberto DiDomenico, who accepted an internship at Reif Estate Winery as a research assistant. Upon his graduation from the University of Guelph in Ontario, the post transformed into a winemaking position. Roberto was no stranger to winemaking, having grown up an amateur winemaker with a wine-producing father. His minimalistic approach to winemaking by "letting the wine make itself" is the perfect complement to Klaus' belief that ultimately nature makes the wine.

Above: The Reif wine boutique, with its signature cupola, was designed to complement the original winery that was housed in an 1870s coach house.

Right: Contemplate the colors, aromas, and flavors used to describe wines in the interpretive wine sensory garden.

Facing Page: A flight of wines awaits at Wine Sensory Bar, one of Niagara's most sophisticated tasting bars.
Photographs courtesy of Reif Estate Winery

Since that time, his flair for red varietals, inspired by time spent in the Bordeaux region of France and travels to Italy, has been revealed. His famed Tesoro took gold at the International Wine and Spirit Competition, followed by the critically acclaimed First Growth Collection of wines, which are produced from the oldest vineyard blocks of the vineyard's terroir.

Today the winery includes a new wine boutique that offers themed flights, blind tastings, and exquisite pairings. A wine sensory garden featuring plantings representative of colors, flavors, and aromas found in differing grape varietals is an ideal location for a leisurely stroll or savoring a glass

of VQA wine and an artisan cheese or charcuterie plate under the arbor. The neighboring Grand Victorian Bed and Breakfast is a 19th-century mansion, offering a complete retreat for visitors, including packages for pre-planned expeditions as well as professional accommodations for winery weddings.

Above: Estate bottled wines from Reif's 125-acre vineyard in the Niagara River sub-appellation.

Facing Page: French barriques and an Italian icewine press create an intimate setting for dinners and events.
Photographs by Steven Elphick

First Growth Cabernet Sauvignon
Pair with filet mignon with peppercorn sauce.

Shiraz Pinot
Pair the kiln-dried wine with any choice of lamb.

Vidal Icewine
Pair with a bold blue cheese.

Tastings
Open to the public daily, year-round

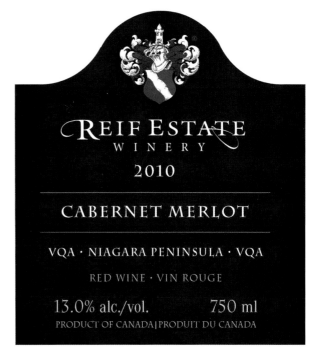

Reimer Vineyards Winery

Niagara-on-the-Lake

It began as a basement hobby. After every harvest, vineyard owner Art Reimer thoughtfully considered the grapes left behind, still clinging to the vine. Art allowed them to hang on a little longer and crushed them for table wine. Joining a local amateur winemaking group called the Niagara Wine Guild nurtured his innate talent and eventual success; winning awards for local amateur competitions fed his passion. He purchased vitis vinifera varietals of chardonnay and Johannisburg riesling in order to expand the vineyard's selections to include European varietals. And so began an onslaught of new plantings, including pinot noir, gewürztraminer, gamay, cabernet sauvignon, cabernet franc, and chambourcin, over the following several years.

The vineyard has been producing grapes long before a winery was constructed. Toiling in the Four Mile Creek sub-appellation land for a quarter of a century, Art began blending wine in his basement, which he eventually outgrew, and then he moved into an onsite barn. Opened on August 1, 2010, Reimer Vineyards Winery is furnished with steel tanks, aging barrels, and cases of vintages; a dream experimentation lab for an engineering and agriculture graduate. Wielding a bachelor of science degree, Art has an aptitude for vineyard practices and winemaking technology that has been enhanced by a career building and maintaining science equipment. His inquisitive nature allows for a superb comprehension of the mechanics behind industry standards and practices, which subsequently led to a chief change in vineyard operations.

Top: Bottles of estate-made vintages are from pesticide-free and hand-processed grapes.

Bottom and Facing Page: The Reimer crest regally greets guests as they arrive at the charming winery and retail store.
Photographs by Steven Elphick

After years of witnessing veteran farmers apply pesticides and chemicals to their crops, Art saw health problems emerge, which motivated him to investigate organic farming methods. Although he had worked the land using accepted methods for a quarter of a century, in 2005 he applied organic practices as well as hand picking, crushing, bottling, corking, and labeling. Additionally, biodiesel fuels the tractors and most everything on the estate is recycled. A sheep occupies the back of all bottles as a symbol of the vineyard's commitment to maintaining organic practices in the future.

The Reimer Vineyards Winery store replicates an old mercantile shop from the 1860s. Inside, visitors may find Art's wife, Sue, stocking bottles of organic red vintages or scheduling overnight stays at the couple's cottage next door. Cozy and quaint, it contains three bedrooms for extended visits, affording wine-loving journeyers a respite from long commutes and delayed relaxation.

Top: Thriving vines have a matchless view of the majestic Niagara Escarpment.

Bottom and Facing Page: Art and Sue Reimer enjoy a glass of estate cabernet and welcome wine lovers to their lush vineyard and quaint retail shop.
Photographs by Steven Elphick

Galahad
(70% pinot noir, 30% gamay)
Pair with a wine-based marinade on steak or lamb shank.

Peace & Harmony
(60% chambourcin, 20% cabernet sauvignon, 20% cabernet franc)
Pair with pork shish kebobs or sausage and peppers.

Cabernet Rosé
Pair with grilled seafood in a lemon-butter sauce.

Tastings
Open to the public daily, seasonally

Southbrook Vineyards

Niagara-on-the-Lake

When Bill and Marilyn Redelmeier think of gourmet cuisine, fine wine aligns harmoniously. As avid lovers of the edible arts, they were inspired in 1991 to create a boutique winery housed in century-old barns. By sourcing some of the region's finest grape varietals, Southbrook Vineyards produced its first 2,000 cases of wine to an eager audience of fellow foodies. An instant hit, the bottles sold rapidly and continued to do so year after year. A decade after its inception, the winery expanded as demand increased, and Bill considered a strategic purchase of land in Niagara that would firmly establish Southbrook in the heart of Ontario's wine country.

In 2005, winemaker and viticulturist Ann Sperling introduced Bill and Marilyn to a 74-acre parcel of land in the warm Four Mile Creek sub-appellation of Niagara-on-the-Lake. Suitably planted with 36 acres of well selected varieties and premium clones, the couple realized the site's potential and relocated the winery while establishing the vineyard with certified organic and biodynamic methods. The family's charming country store and pumpkin patch remain in Richmond Hill. That same year, the Redelmeiers commissioned Toronto-based Jack Diamond, principal of Diamond and Schmidt Architects, to design a world-class winery that would both honor vineyard life and sit lightly on the land. The resulting structure sensibly stores celebrated vintages for discerning clientele within an awe-worthy interior. Hosting private parties, elegant weddings, and corporate events, the certified LEED Gold structure astounds family, friends, and colleagues with its state-of-the-art design. Recipient of the coveted International Architecture Award—sponsored by the European Center for Architecture, Art, Design, and Urban Studies—the building offers three exquisite spaces for an assortment of rendezvous.

Top: Poetica, the winery's flagship brand, is only produced in the finest vintages.

Bottom: Southbrook's OXO line racking system combines beauty with practicality.

Facing Page: The west façade of the hospitality pavilion provides a spectacular welcome for incoming guests.
Photographs by Steven Elphick

An expansive glass hospitality pavilion set against a 200-meter-long, three-meter-high landscape wall marks the entrance to the winery and salutes Niagara-on-the-Lake's wine district. The wall is a periwinkle blue incarnation that anchors the light-filled pavilion into the vine-covered landscape, conforming well to every season. Inside, recessed wine displays, storage, and a wine library with elevated glass vaults containing aging barrels further the enchanting experience.

The grandest of them all, the great room is a large space that revels in copious light, courtesy of floor-to-ceiling windows. A demonstration kitchen blooms into the room and suggests an epicurean activity accompanied by selections of wine from the library just behind. Beautifully backlit niches as well as a glass barrel-vault wall insert simple beauty into the space.

The Oak Room, positioned at the heart of the building, is a point of convergence for the winery's circulating energy and design. Its spherical elements juxtapose the linear continuity found throughout the rest of the building, underscored by recurring circles found within chairs, exposed wine barrels, a table, wine glasses, wine bottles, and even racks. The oak used for the table was hand selected by Bill from his historic family farm and made into a stunning showpiece that accommodates 14 for tastings and intimate dinners. In the summer, an outdoor pizza oven entices people to linger, enjoying local food and a glass of wine.

Above: The dramatic east façade at dusk showcases the interior hospitality pavilion.

Right: The Oak Room, with its grand table, is the perfect place for intimate gatherings.

Facing Page: The great room hosts tastings, elegant dinners, meetings, and cooking demonstrations.
Photographs by Steven Elphick

Biodynamic farming emphasizes balance and coordination between soil, plants, and animals to grow low-impact, vibrant crops such as grapes. Applying farming methods that use specially prepared composts, filled with natural ingredients such as herbal teas, the winery reaps superior results, creating fine wines worthy of being cellared. Varieties such as merlot, chardonnay, cabernet franc, cabernet sauvignon, vidal, syrah, and petit verdot ripen in time above enigmatic soil.

Top: The sheep bring harmony and fertility to the vineyard.

Bottom: Special teas for biodynamic preparations nurture the vineyard.

Facing Page: The forest behind the vineyard is an important part of the property.
Photographs by Steven Elphick

Director of winemaking and viticulture Ann Sperling collaborates with vineyard manager Scott Jones to produce five labels of vintages under the Southbrook brand. Assisted by associate winemaker Brian Hamilton, Ann crafts wines for each series—Triomphe, Poetica, Whimsy!, and Connect, as well as Icewine and Framboise—with a variety of palates in mind. While each product family offers a heightened regional experience, the Whimsy! series includes limited-production wines made exclusively each season. Triomphe is the brand's signature series, appealing to reserve-loving consumers, while Poetica and Connect are greatly admired as well. Many of Southbrook's wines have won medals worldwide and the team is especially proud of securing the Organic Innovators Award. With all of the charted distinctions, ranging from color to notes to label design, all of the bottles share a common purpose: to encourage and ignite conversation with family and friends, creating future memories ripe with nostalgia.

Top: The retail space is elegant.

Middle: Bill and Marilyn Redelmeier have championed local products for more than 30 years.

Bottom: A selection of Southbrook's wine families: Whimsy!, Poetica, and Connect.

Facing Page: The Southbrook wall creates a dramatic entrance to the property.
Photographs by Steven Elphick

Triomphe Cabernet Franc Rosé
Pair with locally raised grilled chicken, tapas, or vegetable paninis.

Poetica Cabernet Merlot
Pair with locally raised beef tenderloin or filet served with roasted red peppers and caramelized onions.

Triomphe Cabernet Franc
Pair with locally raised beef ribs braised in a cabernet sauce.

Triomphe Chardonnay
Pair with chicken or seafood alfredo.

Tastings
Open daily, year-round

Stratus Vineyards
Niagara-on-the-Lake

In homage to the estate's layered soil and namesake cloud cover, Stratus Vineyards' wines offer a complexity and beauty reflective of the terroir from which they come. Proudly established on some of the oldest farmed agricultural land in Canada, Stratus' 62-acre Niagara-on-the-Lake estate is home to 18 grape varieties and produces some of the region's favorite wines under the Stratus, Tollgate, and Wildass labels.

Made from 100-percent estate-grown, hand-tended grapes, Stratus' signature wines—Stratus Red and Stratus White—reintroduce wine lovers to the tradition of assemblage, or the art of combining several grape varieties into a single wine. These two signature wines capture the essence of the vineyard, and the winery's annual batches of small-lot varietals, including popular icewines, continue Stratus' exciting winemaking tradition.

Stratus has come by a reputation as one of the world's most interesting wineries to visit. The tasting rooms are a study in Venetian plaster, sandblasted and rift-cut oak, and end-cut mesquite paneling. The cozy-but-cool vibe attracts wine lovers who are drawn to Stratus' curated style and trademark innovation.

Inside the facility, virtually every piece of equipment can be reconfigured in response to winemaking demands. Even equipment as basic as the hand-sorting tables can be set up in multiple ways to accommodate the needs of that day's harvest. Instead of using traditional pumping methods, which can introduce air and compromise flavors, Stratus wines flow naturally—by means of gravity and a four-story elevator tank—from stainless steel or oak fermenters into carefully selected French oak barrels in the winery's bright, airy, above-ground, 1,000-barrel cellar. There, under the care of Stratus' winemaking team, the wines

Top: The terrace is particularly tranquil at sunset.

Bottom: Barrel selections await the art of assemblage.

Facing Page: The vineyards glow at sunrise.
Photographs by Steven Elphick

age behind translucent panels that not only separate the cellar from the rest of the facility but also allow in precious natural light. Carefully monitored geothermal cooling keeps the cellar at an ideal 14° C.

It should come as no surprise that Stratus was the world's first fully LEED-certified winery. Architect Les Andrew and interior designer Diego Burdi designed the building to function as a physical manifestation of the winery's philosophy. The Zen-minimalist architecture is a study in the theory that form follows function, and the building and systems were designed with a "loose fit for a long life" philosophy. Great architecture and planning may be the estate's calling card, but a winery is nothing without a great artist tending the vines and barrels. Winemaker Jean-Laurent (J-L) Groux is the mastermind behind both the vineyard and winemaking operations.

Above: The Stratus tasting flight.

Right: The Press Alley with overhead oak fermenters.

Facing Page: The Vineyard tasting room overlooks the barrel cellar, terrace, and vines.
Photographs by Steven Elphick

A native of France's Loire Valley, J-L honed his winemaking skills in the vineyards of Burgundy and Bordeaux, venerating the traditions of winemaking but choosing not to be bound by them. Instead he continually experiments with fresh ideas, these days in collaboration with winemaking consultant Paul Hobbs, while pursuing the very traditional goal of creating outstanding, age-worthy wines that embody the essence of the vineyard. His insistence on a long hang time—Stratus' cabernet grapes are often left on the vine until early December—plays a significant role in his success. His methods of drastic thinning, low yields, and an extended extraction may seem painstaking and unorthodox from the outside, but the proof is on the palate, and Stratus' results are inarguable.

Above Left and Facing Page: Stratus Vineyards has been LEED accredited since opening in 2005.

Above Right: Stratus Red and Stratus White are winery signatures.

Left: Winemaker J-L Groux ensures quality in every bottle.
Photographs by Steven Elphick

Stratus White
Divine with seared Lake Erie pickerel garnished with morels, Vichy carrots, dried bacon, and wild watercress.

Stratus Red
Pair with a savory Cumbrae Farms beef strip loin and serve with morel mushrooms, white asparagus, and a rich Béarnaise sauce.

Stratus Cabernet Franc
Perfect alongside shepherd's pie made from a braised lamb shank ragout, roasted root vegetables, and buttery potato purée.

Stratus Icewine Red
Delicious with a dark chocolate tart topped with wild Ontario blueberries, burnt almonds, and crème Anglaise.

Tastings
Open daily, year-round

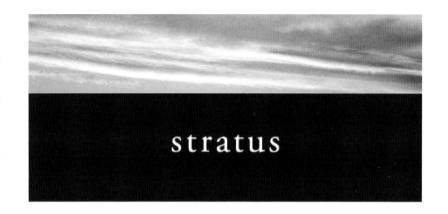

Strewn

Niagara-on-the-Lake

The origin for Strewn's name is an Old English adjective meaning "spread" or "scattered." Chosen for its strong phonetics and lack of connotation, it seemed appropriate for a New World winery, one that would need its own exclusive autonomy. The collaborative effort of a husband-and-wife team and a seasoned industry veteran, the winery opened its doors in the summer of 1997 and has grown in both size and stature, as evidenced by the accumulation of more than 150 international and national awards, a strong presence at the LCBO, and exports to more than a dozen countries.

Strewn's 10-acre property was formerly a sprawling cannery used to process local peaches, cherries, plums, apricots, and tomatoes for market. As an induction into a second life, the building underwent an extensive renovation and rebuild. Reflecting an agricultural-industrial exterior, the winery is an engaging attraction that offers one of Niagara's most in-depth visitor experiences, including a retail boutique, tasting room, recreational cooking school, and restaurant. Soaring 35 feet high, an atrium bathed in light beckons visitors to enter.

From its infancy, Strewn has produced well-crafted wines that showcase the region's superb terroir and simultaneously enrich the local food and wine scene. Grapes from the winery's lakeshore and inland vineyards, along with those purchased from a handful of other growers, are crafted into structured, age-worthy, Bordeaux-style reds and refreshing whites. More than 30 VQA-certified wines—some for sale only at the winery—are available for tasting in the winery boutique, including trophy-winning icewines and red blends like Strewn Three, a classic mix of merlot, cabernet sauvignon, and cabernet franc.

Top: The atrium is a key focal point of the architecture, providing access to the tasting room, retail boutique, cooking school, and restaurant.

Bottom: Strewn wines have won major awards in Canada and Europe.

Facing Page: Strewn is housed in a repurposed fruit cannery that dates back to the 1940s. Extensive renovations to create the visitor center included use of the original block and a similar metal roof.
Photographs by Steven Elphick

Snagging a coveted Grand Gold at VinItaly, an icewine trophy at the International Wine Challenge, and a gold medal at the International Challenge du Vin in France shows just how highly regarded the winery is.

Strewn is also recognized for the Wine Country Cooking School, Canada's first cooking school to be located at a winery, which offers hands-on classes and culinary vacations for recreational cooks. Focusing on the harmonious relationship between food and wine, the school showcases an abundance of locally grown fresh produce in the seasonal three-course meals

made by participants during classes. For guests who wish to get right to the eating, the onsite restaurant, Terroir La Cachette, features Provençal-inspired dishes made from fresh, regional ingredients.

Above: The Wine Country Cooking School at Strewn offers one-day hands-on classes, seasonal culinary weekends, and five-day culinary vacations for recreational cooks.

Right: Participants prepare three-course meals with seasonal ingredients, many from local growers, while learning about food and wine pairing.

Facing Page Top: The restaurant at Strewn, open for both lunch and dinner, provides a warm, welcoming dining atmosphere. The menu features local ingredients with a Provençal touch.

Facing Page Bottom: Winemakers Marc Bradshaw and Joe Will, who both studied winemaking in Australia, are committed to producing premium wines from grapes grown in the Niagara Peninsula.
Photographs by Steven Elphick

Each season, Strewn hosts a series of in-the-vineyard and winery activities. From pruning back the dormant vines in late winter to a green harvest in ripe summer months, the popular crush in the fall to a winter wine harvest followed by an icewine festival in January, guests are included in winery life and encouraged to participate in important events year-round. Special tasting flights, food and wine pairings, and pre-release celebrations are just as beloved but far less laborious than the vineyard adventures, and a winemaker's dinner twice a year is known to surpass expectations.

Strewn also offers a membership program called The Barrel Club, where members can enjoy elite access to exclusive perks such as having your own wine barrel—in French, Canadian, or American oak—that will forever display your name. Not only does the association come with exclusive bragging rights, but members and friends are also invited to special Barrel Club events and tastings. After three years the empty barrel can be carted home for an ultimate keepsake or it can be filled again with more divine wine.

Top: The winery is set amidst vineyards and orchards. Grapes grown on the property include gewürztraminer, sauvignon blanc, and pinot blanc.

Middle: Gewürztraminer, a grape used to make white wines, is distinguished by its bronze color and wonderful floral and fruity aromas.

Bottom: Wines in Strewn's Terroir label are of outstanding quality, while the popular TwoVines label denotes affordable, easy-drinking wines.

Facing Page: Strewn's barrel cellar contains more than 400 barrels—a combination of American, Canadian, and French oak—used to age white and red wines.
Photographs by Steven Elphick

WINE & FARE

Strewn Sauvignon Blanc
Pair with mixed greens with fresh mint vinaigrette, tomatoes, and sheep's milk feta.

Strewn Cabernet Franc
Pair with grilled, butterflied pork tenderloin with ginger, soy, and sesame.

Strewn Chardonnay Barrel Fermented Terroir
Pair with salmon, caramelized onions, and Swiss chard strudel.

Strewn Cabernet Select Late Harvest
Pair with individual molten chocolate cakes with Niagara raspberry coulis.

Tastings
Open to the public daily, year-round

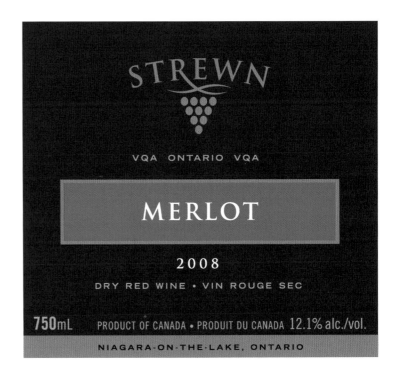

STREWN

VQA ONTARIO VQA

MERLOT

2008

DRY RED WINE · VIN ROUGE SEC

750mL   PRODUCT OF CANADA · PRODUIT DU CANADA 12.1% alc./vol.

NIAGARA-ON-THE-LAKE, ONTARIO

Thirty Bench Winemakers

Beamsville

In Beamsville Bench, a small sub-appellation of the Niagara Peninsula, sits a charming cottage-style building amid sloping rows of some of Ontario's more exclusive grapevines: Thirty Bench Winemakers. Founded by a group of passionate winemakers including Tom Muckle, Yorgos Papageorgiou, and Frank Zeritsch, Thirty Bench specializes in the production of small-lot, small-batch rieslings from some of the oldest vines in the region.

Thirty Bench's vines are custom grown—cropped and thinned by hand—to yield a small lot of grapes for production. Winemaker Emma Garner and estate manager Fiona Muckle oversee the growth of Thirty Bench's rieslings as well as an array of other varietals: pinot gris, gewürztraminer, chardonnay, rosé, pinot noir, cabernet tranc, merlot, and cabernet sauvignon. The winery's philosophy revolves around the less-is-more concept when it comes to balancing out yield and quality in its wines. Guests are welcome to stop by daily for tastings, or schedule personalized tasting and riesling vineyard tours on weekends. Further promoting the exclusivity of its fine wines, Thirty Bench offers a limited number of memberships to its No. 30 wine club, for those who have a great passion for Ontario wines.

Top: Thirty Bench produces premium wines grown from estate vineyards on the Beamsville Bench, a superior grape growing region on the Niagara Peninsula.

Middle: The wines are carefully crafted by winemaker Emma Garner in small lots, ensuring every single bottle of Thirty Bench wine boasts exceptional quality and flavor.

Bottom: Thirty Bench focuses on what the vineyard does best: growing riesling and classic red varietals on vines managed for low yield and maximum fruit intensity.

Facing Page: The tasting room features impeccable views.
Photographs by Steven Elphick

Trius Winery at Hillebrand

Niagara-on-the-Lake

Trius Winery at Hillebrand sits on a gorgeous piece of fertile land in the heart of Niagara-on-the-Lake. Specializing in a red blend comprised of three varietals—cabernet franc, cabernet sauvignon, and merlot—Trius has quickly made a name for itself and become the producer of one of the best known red wines in Canada. Winemaker Craig McDonald, along with estate manager Michelle Brisebois, oversees the production of Trius's specialty: sparkling wines.

In addition to its sparkling wines, Trius produces chardonnay, riesling, cabernet franc, cabernet sauvignon, merlot, and rosé. The winery sits in the middle of a one-acre estate vineyard and partners with over 30 growers from across the Niagara Peninsula. Annually, it hosts the music event Trius Jazz & Blues at the Winery. Various dinners—under the direction of winery chef Frank Dodd—are presented to guests periodically throughout the year. The partnership of fine wine and quality fare is paramount to the Trius Winery at Hillebrand experience. Trius is open to the public daily and features extended hours on weekends in addition to special events.

Top: Trius wines crafted by winemaker Craig McDonald have set the benchmark for exceptional winemaking since the winery's inception in 1989 with the release of Trius Red.

Middle: Chef Frank Dodd focuses on innovative seasonal menus in a spectacular setting in the heart of the winery.

Bottom: Guests enjoy a range of wine experiences, from vineyard excursions to the interactive blend your own Trius Red.

Facing Page: Barrel cellar dinners are a favorite of visitors.
Photographs by Steven Elphick

Vignoble Rancourt Winery

Niagara-on-the-Lake

As the old adage goes, good things come in small packages. Beautifully illustrated by Vignoble Rancourt Winery—a petite vineyard and winery situated near the merging of Lake Ontario and the Niagara River—the story began as a hand-planted project completed by a passionate husband and his devoted wife. Bottling 800 cases of wine annually—most of which are subject to selling out—the estate represents Lionel and Lorraine Rancourt's realized desire for retirement on rural grounds, raising grapes over vine-strung hills.

A historical downtown area attracting year-round tourism while preserving a small-town pace seemed to be a prime location for a nearby vineyard. Within Niagara-on-the-Lake's sub-appellation, Lionel and Lorraine settled land, just as they had in Quebec years prior, and spent the following eight years planning, planting, and growing the vines. In 2005, Vignoble Rancourt Winery was officially bonded and a new winery facility echoing the effortless yet romantic style of the Rancourt's rustic French heritage followed just one year later.

The winery's timeless post and beam barn-like structure is cleverly clad in cream-toned stone and taupe wood paneling. With one level designated for general tastings and another reserved for private parties, the space can comfortably accommodate crowds of consumers that venture to the estate each week. A neighboring bed and breakfast, La Residence Rancourt, offers a cozy motel alternative for up to eight overnight guests at a time. Homey sleeping quarters and a hot breakfast in the morning are reminiscent of family hospitality, which elevates the estate to a destination status.

Top: A row of peach trees nods to the land's previous life, resilient nature, and promising soil.

Bottom: A few vines of Sovereign Coronation table grapes are a sign of the coming harvest that increases anticipation.

Facing Page: The winery's stone and wood veneer is complementary to every season, while its French-inspired, barn-like frame charms ordinary visitors into confirmed Francophiles daily.
Photographs by Steven Elphick

Rooted in deltaic sands and silt-based soils, the vineyard excels at merlot, cabernet sauvignon, cabernet franc, riesling, and chardonnay varietals due to a fair climate and nearby body of fresh water. One of the most popular blends is Meritage—a medium-bodied Bordeaux style made from cabernet sauvignon, cabernet franc, and merlot with bold blackberry and coffee tastes—which appeals to mature palates that enjoy smooth, tannic, and spicy notes. Another favorite, Noble Blanc, is a mingling of riesling and chardonnay with tones of pineapple, citrus, and honey—a white wine lover's paradise. Both selections receive warranted interest, along with fellow collection favorites, and should be enjoyed with flattering cuisine to maximize flavors.

A true achievement, Rancourt's vineyard and winery required an ardent heart and sovereign hands to establish. After spending 10 years doing what he loved most with the person he cherished above all else, Lionel unexpectedly passed away on December 30, 2007, just one year after the winery's opening. A loyal husband for 47 years and a fervent cultivator, he is forever memorialized within the name, walls, and roots of the property.

Above: Soft walnut floors, caramel walls, and ambient lighting welcome group tastings and private parties to a designated space upstairs.

Right: The Rancourt family tree tells the courageous story of 12 generations who emigrated from France and began anew in Canada.

Facing Page Top: A knowledgeable and enthusiastic staff welcomes guests into the warm tasting room for savored tastes of boutique-style wine. With a bit of luck, Lorraine may serve you herself.

Facing Page Bottom: Estate specialties, such as cabernet sauvignon, merlot, and other Bordeaux blends, are available at the tasting room and also online.
Photographs by Steven Elphick

Above: A native of Spain, Joseph Enrich was raised with an authentic passion for great wines, which is evident with the success he's achieved as Rancourt's winemaker. Co-founded by Lorraine and Lionel Rancourt in 2005, the winery continues to be one of Niagara's top contenders.

Loft: Extended daylight and moderately cool temperatures lengthen the growing season, which is ideal for white varietals such as riesling, sauvignon blanc, and chardonnay.
Photographs by Steven Elphick

Continuing Lionel's dream and grape growing excellence, his wife Lorraine, sons Marcel and Dennis, and daughter Carole have exquisitely combined winemaking excellence from France with rural tradition from Quebec to create fine wines from Niagara. The newest addition to the team, winemaker Jean-Pierre Colas, almost instantly fell in love with Rancourt's charming character as well as its commitment to French traditional winemaking that still utilizes modern equipment. Naturally talented and well educated, he was previously employed by the prestigious Domaine Laroche Chablis in France as head winemaker for almost a decade. That experience, plus years of exploring appellations and working for wineries in Chile, Argentina, and New Zealand, made him a prime candidate for the position. With meticulous skill, he crafts elite bottles of limited wine, such as the estate specialty, icewine, which is a delicate blend of cabernet sauvignon and cabernet franc juices extracted from frozen grapes to create a perfect union of sweet and tangy flavors like strawberry, rhubarb, and honey-laced fruit. Jean-Pierre's partnership honors Rancourt's reputation in name and wine.

Top and Bottom: Shiraz vines, along with a number of others, thrive in Niagara's idyllic environment.

Facing Page: Breezes from the lake keep the flag in flight and ventilate the vines, ensuring cool, gently maturing grapes that retain fruitiness and acidity.
Photographs by Steven Elphick

Meritage
Pair with Gorgonzola cheese and smoked bacon on steak burgers.

Noble Blanc
Pair with baked stuffed lobster and lemon-dipped asparagus.

Icewine
Pair with raspberry cheesecake or any flavor of whipped mousse.

Tastings
Open to the public daily, year-round

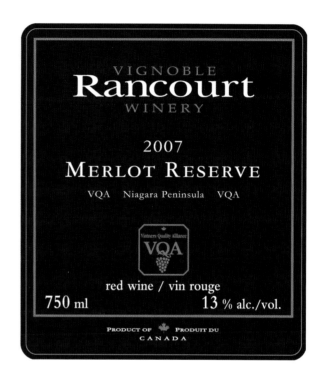

VIGNOBLE
Rancourt
WINERY

2007
MERLOT RESERVE

VQA   Niagara Peninsula   VQA

Vintners Quality Alliance
VQA

red wine / vin rouge

750 ml   13 % alc./vol.

PRODUCT OF ❦ PRODUIT DU
CANADA

Crown Bench Estates Winery, page 130

Le Clos Jordanne, page 158

Flat Rock Cellars, page 134

NIAGARA ESCARPMENT
AND TWENTY VALLEY

13th Street Winery

St. Catharines

Founded in 1998 by four career professionals and award-winning amateur winemakers, 13th Street Winery began as a serious hobby. It produced fewer than 2,000 cases per year for a decade, until orderly lines extended out the tasting room door and many fans went home empty-handed. In order to temper this supply-and-demand dilemma, John Mann and Doug Whitty joined 13th Street Winery as new partners in 2006 and subsequently became sole owners of the winery two years later. In the years since, 13th Street Winery has grown into a respected producer of more than 13,000 cases per year, and the company philosophy of creating small lots of estate-grown, handcrafted table and sparkling wines from the best grapes remains unchanged even today.

13th Street Winery strives for harmony, balance, and sustainability when it comes to crafting its VQA-certified Estate, Reserve, Old Vines, and Essence series of wines. Believing that wine is a full expression of the land, the team pays vigilant attention to canopy management, pruning, yield management, and timely harvesting, followed by hand-picking and sorting grapes from the Creek Shores and Four Mile Creek sub-appellations in the Niagara Peninsula. By doing so, premium varietals such as chardonnay, sauvignon blanc, riesling, merlot, gamay, and syrah receive less imposition from foreign influences and the character of the fruit is unaltered. Gentle manipulation does begin in the winery, where mainly French and select American oak barrels—along with stainless steel tanks—enhance the development of the wines during production. However, these methods would not add dimension to wines that didn't already possess adequate fruit character from the beginning.

Top: *The Necklace* features five components, each representing of a different element in the life of the artist, Karoly Veres. Visitors to the winery are invited to wander through the grounds and view all the sculptures on display.

Bottom: Grape leaves in the fall.

Facing Page: The front entrance to the winery is highlighted by *Margo*, a white marble sculpture by artist Karoly Veres. *Photographs by Steven Elphick*

Devout advocates of blending, those at 13th Street Winery often experiment with new techniques, barrels, or vineyard blocks in hopes of capturing an undiscovered collaboration of variables. Leading the team is Jean-Pierre Colas, head winemaker and a native of France who, understandably, feels wine flowing through his veins. Jean-Pierre joined the team in 2009, working alongside winery co-founder and former winemaker Herb Jacobson. In 2010, Herb retired and Jean-Pierre took over full-time winemaking duties. With more than two decades of experience honed in Canada, France, Chile, and New Zealand, Jean Pierre stepped into the position with refined skills and technique. He most notably worked for the prestigious Chablis house Domaine Laroche, where he oversaw production for a decade, the benefits of which are still coming to fruition.

Another important addition to the winery came in 2009, when a state-of-the-art production and hospitality facility with high-end winemaking equipment and additional estate vineyards opened on Fourth Avenue. Greenhouses and plantings thrive on the 25-acre estate, the former home of the Brucedale Gardens, including new plantings of riesling, pinot noir, and gamay.

Transcending the expected, 13th Street Winery engages all of the senses at every opportunity, from fine sculptures gracing the grounds to a renovated turn-of-the-century farmhouse presenting stimulating art. A spectacular gallery waits inside, where some

Left: Cold- and moisture-sensitive pinot noir vines grow in a classic hoop house for protection from the elements.

Facing Page Top and Middle: The focal point of the gallery room is the majestic 18-foot, 1,300-pound solid slab table made from sustainable Indonesian hardwood. The artwork found inside 13th Street Winery is rotated throughout the year and features original works by various Canadian artists.

Facing Page Bottom: The wraparound veranda is perfect for enjoying a glass of 13th Street wine in the pastoral setting.
Photographs by Steven Elphick

of Canada's most respected artists, such as William Ronald, Michael Adamson, and David Bolduc, exhibit their work. The rotating pieces are displayed in a room whose floor-to-ceiling windows stun and a majestic, 18-foot Kayu Meh table made from Indonesian hardwood begs to be touched. Its long body can comfortably accommodate up to 22 guests, ideal for private dinner parties or corporate events held in the presence of local and original artwork.

Continuing with the complete sensorial experience, the bakery and marketplace is conveniently located across from the wine store and tasting bar. Its heavenly scents range from fresh and local fruits, vegetables, and flowers to tempting baked goods like artisan flatbread pizzas, tarts, and pies. The shop contains nature's confections direct from Whitty Farms, which was established in 1908 and is the sister company of the winery. Its artisan cheese and charcuterie boards are a summertime favorite, compiled for visitors to enjoy while reclining on the wraparound veranda or exploring the vibrant and fragrant gardens. Non-perishable merchandise like kitchen tools, books, and jewelry make for timeless keepsakes and thoughtful gifts for family and friends, while jams, jellies, preserves, tapenades, and oils can be perfectly packaged to take home and enjoy year-round.

Top: 13th Street's signature wines include traditional method sparkling wines and the Gamay series.

Bottom: Artisan cheese and charcuterie boards are offered during the summer months.

Facing Page: The full-length windows in the winery's gallery room offer guests a spectacular view of the gardens and wooded area.
Photographs by Steven Elphick

Grande Cuvée Blanc de Noirs Brut
Pair with Atlantic salmon gravlax with buckwheat blinis
and lemon crème fraîche.

Chardonnay Sandstone Vineyard Reserve
Pair with butter-poached Nova Scotia lobster ravioli with fried sage.

Gamay Noir Sandstone Vineyard Old Vines
Pair with Lyonnaise sausage with Le Puy lentils and warm potato salad.

Syrah Essence
Pair with a roasted leg of lamb with black olive and caper tapenade.

Tastings
Open to the public Monday through Saturday, year-round

Alvento Winery
Vineland

I talian Bruno Moos and his wife Elyane Grenier began making wine in Soiana, a hillside town in Tuscany, about three decades ago. Determined to establish a reputable vineyard that would someday become a full winery, they began on four hectares of land in the heart of Italy's wine country. The couple prospered tremendously in the touristy town, and after a number of years had passed they decided to relocate to Canada, where the virgin terroir was receiving praise for producing distinctive fruit with unique flavor. With wine connoisseur and new partner Morrie Neiss, they acquired a 16-acre waterfront estate positioned on Niagara's peninsula and called it Alvento, meaning "at the wind" in Italian. Just on the west side of the Jordan Harbor, Alvento Winery rests on layers of clay, silts, and sands and is said to be a part of the largest and most distinguishable viticultural area in Canada.

The region's well developed fruit is largely attributed to cooler temperatures in the summer months, which allow the grapes to reach their maximum maturity. Wintertime, however, proves less beneficial. Although the vineyard was planted in 2001, freezing temperatures during consecutive growing seasons at Alvento prevented a vintage until 2006. The winery—further delayed—was opened in 2009 and mirrors a rustic barn-like structure. Well worth the wait, its inviting nature oozes unpretentious energy, keeping the primary focus on the robust Bordeaux blends for which the region is known.

Top: The large and dark fruit found on the nebbiolo vine is packed with tannic flavors from bold acids. Popular culture attributes the grape's name to either nebbia, meaning "fog" in Italian, which references the skin's foggy exterior, or nobile, meaning "noble" in Italian.

Bottom: Made from the nebbiolo grape, a rarely imported Italian varietal, Alvento's beloved Aria resembles garnets in a glass and offers a bold, full-bodied flavor.

Facing Page: The loft can be reserved for private events and tastings.
Photographs by Steven Elphick

Prepared to be enjoyed with food, red wines such as Elige, Emilie, Aria, and Sondra receive traditional vinification and fermentation in temperature-regulated stainless steel tanks followed by an aging process of 18 to 20 months in oak barrels. Viognier, the estate white, is similarly processed by hand-picking the grapes and gently pressing them for juice prior to clarification; once clarified, they are fermented in both new French oak barrels and stainless steel tanks to optimize individual flavor.

According to the Moos, a good bottle of wine is detected by the second glass. If the second glass is noticeably acidic and bitter, there is no need to finish it. Contrary to that, if the second glass is smooth and flavorful, it should be completed along with the accompanying meal. As Bruno professes, "A good wine consumed in good company brings pleasure, and at the end of the meal, the whole world looks better."

Top and Middle: Bordeaux varietals such as SAR or Second Avenue Red are ideally aged in French barriques—large oak barrels from France—for 18 to 24 months.

Bottom and Facing Page: Winery owners Bruno and Elyane Moos invite wine-loving patrons to their picturesque property each week. The old barn-turned-winery's rustic charm is punctuated by generous views of the surrounding countryside and Eden-like setting.
Photographs by Steven Elphick

Elige
(65% cabernet sauvignon, 33% merlot, 2% cabernet franc)
Pair with an antipasti plate of Camembert, Brie, Gorgonzola, prosciutto, and salami.

Emilie
(70% cabernet franc, 30% merlot)
Pair with roasted lamb, grilled asparagus, and arugula seared in olive oil.

Sondra
(90% merlot, 10% cabernet franc)
Pair with duck smothered in red pepper cream sauce over mushroom risotto.

Tastings
Open to the public, seasonally

Calamus Estate Winery

Jordan

Nestled among the Great Lakes is Calamus Estate Winery, a quaint winery housed in refurbished, 19th-century barns purchased by Derek Saunders and Pat Latin from what was an old family-owned dairy farm. Not unlike the pioneering family who built these dairy barns—one in the 1820s and the second in 1888—the new owners discovered that every new venture demands hard work. Fueled by the romantic dream of owning their own wine business, with the goal to live out their working retirement in an idyllic rural setting, the couple was undaunted by the numerous challenges involved in starting a winery. With every step, a sense of pride was its own reward for Derek and Pat and when the first vintages were produced in 2004, the couple's dream began to reach fruition. In the summer of 2006, Calamus Estate Winery celebrated the opening of its retail store.

By adopting the name Calamus, the Latin word for "arrow," the winery pays homage to the history of Ontario and acknowledges the many arrowhead fragments and stone tools discovered in the surrounding area. Visitors—many of whom arrive via a driving or cycling tour or while hiking the neighboring Bruce Trail—feel the pull of nostalgia from the moment they walk onto the property. Guests easily connect with nature by using the outdoor decks and picnic areas or even strolling through the 20-acre ravine. The rustic building has a second-floor event room, a welcoming spot for private functions, tour groups, corporate meetings, and winemakers' dinners. Guests who attend events on clear nights are often treated to a viewing of the stars with the 16-inch-deep space telescope at the facility's Chronos observatory. And if that is not enough to satisfy visitors' entertainment desires, every September Calamus hosts Fallstock, an annual wine, food, and music festival.

Top: Scenic Ball's Falls and the conservation area are adjacent to the winery.

Bottom: The production barn, originally built around 1820, houses the modern stainless tanks and a selection of French and American oak barrels.

Facing Page: A viewing through the Chronos telescope is a treat enjoyed at many evening events.
Photographs by Steven Elphick

From its two vineyards—one in the Lincoln Lakeshore appellation and another at the winery's location in Vinemount Ridge—Calamus produces a wide array of varietals. These include pinot gris, chardonnay, riesling, gewürztraminer, vidal, cabernet franc, cabernet sauvignon, and merlot. Many of the wines have received special recognition thanks to the unfailing talents of winemaker Arthur Harder. The winery's specialty, pinot gris, truly shines with 17 awards won during the production of its first five vintages. Calamus was also ranked as an InterVin Top 10 winery in 2010. The Vinemount Ridge appellation is fast becoming known for its quality riesling, and Calamus offers both straight varietals and blends. By embracing the natural world around it, the winery offers visitors an experience unique to the region. Very rustic, very scenic, and very good wine!

Top: The labels for Calamus' award-winning wines always feature the archer, Calvin, whose name is an amalgamation of "Cal" for Calamus and "vin" for wine.

Middle Left: Visitors can expect to be greeted by owners Derek and Pat.

Middle Right: A 200-year-old post in the tasting room displays several of the medals won by Calamus Estate Winery.

Bottom: The old hay loft above the tasting room is now a warm and friendly space for large tasting groups and private functions.

Facing Page: Healthy clusters of pinot gris grapes growing alongside the winery can be seen on a sunny day in September.
Photographs by Steven Elphick

Gewürztraminer
Perfect with curry-ginger carrot soup and Vietnamese mango rolls with spicy ginger sauce.

Unoaked Chardonnay
Pairs well with panko-crusted wild salmon on a bed of tarragon, leek, and sweet corn risotto.

Pinot Gris
Flawless with chili-lime chicken kabobs, scallops with white wine sauce, fruit salads, trout amandine, or Indian pork satay.

Cabernet Sauvignon
Superb with Moroccan lamb tagine.

Tastings
Open to the public Thursday through Monday during the off season and daily May through mid-October

CALAMUS
ESTATE WINERY

Crown Bench
Estates Winery

Beamsville

Livia Sipos and Peter Kocsis are the proud owners of Crown Bench Estates Winery. Located on the Beamsville Bench in Niagara, the property has a magnificent view of Lake Ontario and is bordered by the Bruce Trail, designated a UNESCO biosphere reserve. Situated between Lake Ontario and Lake Erie, Crown Bench enjoys a microclimate similar to many great wine regions of the world; it also boasts the same latitude as France and Northern California.

Crown Bench has some of the oldest vinifera vines in Ontario. Planted in the mid '60s with cabernet franc, cabernet sauvignon, chardonnay, pinot noir, and merlot, the vineyards thrive in their idyllic setting. Beyond these more traditional wines, Crown Bench has experimented quite a bit with flavored icewines to develop signatures like Hot Ice and Chocolate Ice, among other unique flavors. All of the winery's ultra-premium wines are the result of fine terroir, biodynamic practices, and hands-on loving care. Truly expressive of the land, each bottle is filled with fruit and love.

Recognized as the best in the province by Ontario's Ministry of Agriculture, the vineyards at Crown Bench yield quality grapes that are transformed into award-winning wines. The winery has earned grand golds at both the International Wine and Spirit Competition in England, for a sauterne, and the Selection Mondiales des Vins, for its innovative chocolate-infused icewine. Its chardonnay is widely regarded as among the best in Ontario. The winery is listed in *Le Guide Hachette des Vins*, an honor claimed by just a handful of Canadian establishments.

Top: Spring brings new promise at the limestone winery entrance.

Bottom: In the fall, a new vintage of cabernet grapes ripen.

Facing Page: The escarpment view is a UNESCO biosphere reserve.
Photographs by Steven Elphick

Beyond outstanding wines, Crown Bench's remarkably scenic property makes it a destination not to be missed. Streams, waterfalls, ponds filled with Canadian geese and ducks, and forests teeming with wildlife complement the acres upon acres of verdant vines. A few vantage points reveal shimmering Lake Ontario and the majesty of downtown Toronto. Whether privately wandering the property, enjoying a tour led by Livia or Peter, or spending time in the tasting room, there are plenty of beautiful and savory elements to discover.

Top and Middle: Ultra-premium gold medal wines represent a promise fulfilled.

Bottom: Owners Livia Sipos and Peter Kocsis toast the Grape King.

Facing Page: The beautiful sloping vineyards produce many varietals of award-winning wine.
Photographs by Steven Elphick

Chardonnay
Serve with smoked salmon and pasta with fresh sauce.

Cabernet Franc
Pair with steak and roast beef.

Hot Ice
Pair with seafood, sushi, and fine cheese of every variety.

Ambrosia
Enjoy as a sinfully delicious dessert.

Tastings
Open to the public daily, year-round

Flat Rock Cellars

Jordan

A trip to France ignited Edward Madronich's passion for wine; today he is the man responsible for Flat Rock Cellars' success. Ed's grandfather tried to obtain a license to own a winery in the 1950s but was denied, so Ed and his father took it upon themselves to make the family dream of owning a winery in Ontario a reality.

Once they laid down the vineyard, they found layers of flat rocks, hence the name of the winery. Flat Rock Cellars is also a reminder that everything comes from the soil. The vineyard-to-table movement is evident in the winery's logo, a woman carrying a basket of grapes as in centuries of old.

Ed explains that the six Ice Ages, the glaciers receding, and the decomposing grass, shrubs, and trees helped create a wonderful limestone bed, ideal for growing flavorful grapes. In addition, Twenty Mile Bench in the Niagara Peninsula offers great drainage and air flow, which are highly favorable to grape growing. The slope and soil are similar to those found in Burgundy, France.

Top: Flat Rock Cellars has a five-level gravity flow winery.

Bottom: Ed Madronich with parents and Flat Rock Cellars founders Nadja Madronich and Ed Madronich Sr.

Facing Page: The retail store and winery are visible from the pinot noir vineyard.
Photographs by Steven Elphick

Nestled between a cerulean blue lake and 80 acres of vineyards are two architecturally stunning buildings with clean modern lines. The winery operates in the best interest of the vine; Ed uses modern techniques and equipment like the ozone machine when he believes they can help improve his production. He favors traditional methods such as hand-picking, hand-sorting, and hand-plunging, which winemakers have been using for centuries for good reason. Flat Rock Cellars specializes in four varietals: chardonnay, pinot noir, riesling, and gewürztraminer.

Most of the winery's practices are environmentally sustainable. The pond generates geothermal heating and cooling to reduce the winery's reliance on fossil fuels and electricity. The five-level gravity flow system processes the wine with minimal handling and pumping, which helps improve its quality. Known for its unprecedented innovation, Flat Rock Cellars was the first in the region to commit 100 percent of production to screw caps.

Above: Flat Rock Cellars' glass-encased winery retail store and tasting bar overlooks the 80-acre estate vineyards.

Right: A few of the cleverly named wines by Flat Rock Cellars.

Facing Page: The modern winery is filled with state-of-the-art stainless steel tanks, individually temperature controlled.
Photographs by Steven Elphick

Ed loves sharing his passion for wine with people and does so in an approachable, friendly way. He tells visitors that if they know what wine they like, they already know a lot about wine. "Wine is like food," he continues, "you know what appeals to your palate." Second only to making great wine, his primary goal is removing the pretense from being a wine enthusiast by making the experience casual and memorable.

When visiting Flat Rock Cellars, be sure to participate in the winery's unique In the Winemaker's Boots experience, which offers a true taste of what it is like to make wine. You will find out firsthand why Ed and his winemaker Ross Wise are so passionate about what they do.

Top: The lush winery gardens greet guests in mid-summer.

Bottom: One of the many inukshuks built by the vintage winemaking teams indicating the end of each year's harvest.

Facing Page: The vineyards at sunrise with the The Rusty Shed—namesake of The Rusty Shed Chardonnay—in the distance.
Photographs by Steven Elphick

Riesling
Pair with pear or tangerine salad.

Nadja's Vineyard Riesling
Sumptuous with lemon-herbed chicken breast and seafood linguini.

Unplugged Chardonnay
Incredible with poached salmon with fresh herbs.

Tastings
Open to the public daily, year-round

FLAT ROCK
CELLARS

The Foreign Affair Winery
Vineland Station

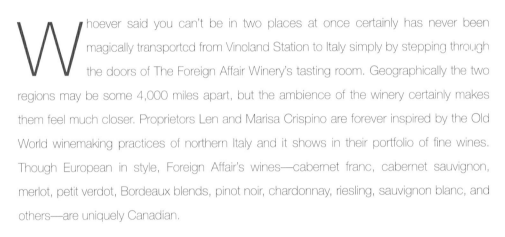

Whoever said you can't be in two places at once certainly has never been magically transported from Vineland Station to Italy simply by stepping through the doors of The Foreign Affair Winery's tasting room. Geographically the two regions may be some 4,000 miles apart, but the ambience of the winery certainly makes them feel much closer. Proprietors Len and Marisa Crispino are forever inspired by the Old World winemaking practices of northern Italy and it shows in their portfolio of fine wines. Though European in style, Foreign Affair's wines—cabernet franc, cabernet sauvignon, merlot, petit verdot, Bordeaux blends, pinot noir, chardonnay, riesling, sauvignon blanc, and others—are uniquely Canadian.

The couple's romance with Italian wine began while they were living with their daughter Stefanie-Marie in Milan as expatriates promoting Canadian trade and investment. As is customary of the Italian seductress, the country lured them in with the simple joys of Italian living and the chance to savor delectable amarone-styled wines prevalent in the area. While many people imagine the winemaking life after visiting, the Crispinos did more than just dream. Driven by the impetus of Len's diagnosis with a life-threatening illness, Marisa decided that it was time for the dream to become reality. Building a life that merged their love of two countries would allow them to feel as though they were in two places at once and provide the energized hope required to forge a successful medical battle.

In 2000, joined by Marisa's brother, Louis, and under the guidance of longtime friend and confidant John Howard, owner of Megalomaniac Wines, the Crispinos made the leap of faith and purchased a prime parcel of fertile Ontario land. In 2001, the vines followed and today 40 healthy acres of amarone-inspired vines grace a southern-facing slope and capture the spirit of northern Italy.

Top: Len Crispino, co-owner of The Foreign Affair Winery, greets guests from a burgundy Vespa.

Bottom: The winery's front doors exclaim "Ciao! Benvenuti a tutti," which is Italian for "Hello! And welcome to all."

Facing Page: The tasting room's Old World style is punctuated by gilded and vaulted ceilings, ornate iron pendants, and a collection of estate vintages protected by heritage doors.
Photographs by Steven Elphick

Not only reminiscent of their Italian muse in atmosphere, the Crispinos' winemaking is inspired by the Old World appassimento grape drying process, which while risky, ultimately adds richness, texture, depth, and complexity to their wines. The Crispinos refer to this approach as "slow wine" because it requires highly time-consuming hand-harvesting to avoid any grape puncturing. Once harvested and hand-transported, the grapes are set to naturally dry on specialized trays for upward of six months. Allowing the grapes to dry decreases the yield of juice but increases the character of the wine, making it rich, styled, and integral.

The Crispinos have introduced and innovatively applied the technique, which is traditionally reserved for red wines, to the craftsmanship of all their wines including the white varietals—a first for the Canadian marketplace. Further, Foreign Affair's Unreasonable cabernet franc grapes spend an uncanny 163 days drying. Given this absolutely unreasonable winemaking practice, the Crispinos drew upon George Bernard Shaw's famous quote: "The reasonable man adapts himself to the conditions that surround him…The unreasonable man adapts surrounding conditions to himself…All progress depends on the unreasonable man" when naming the singular wine.

Top: Winery patrons celebrate their wedding anniversary with a rare bottle of Unreasonable—a cabernet franc—while on a cruise.
Photograph courtesy of The Foreign Affair Winery

Bottom and Facing Page: Proud proprietors of The Foreign Affair Winery Len, Marisa, and Louie present ripe bunches of estate grapes, which become delectable wines that fill artfully labeled estate bottles.
Photographs by Steven Elphick

Fans of Foreign Affair wines can supplement their passion through the winery's Conspiracy Council, a community of "conspirators" who, in one way or another, have helped shape or have been shaped by the winery's goals, beliefs, and inspiration. Self directed, this council acts as a sounding board to promote the spirit of the winery.

At times philosophical, Len attempts to deliver important life messages through the wine they craft. The designs on the bottles, which recently won a gold medal in San Francisco, capture Len's idea that we must always appreciate what we have in our lives. Marisa, whom he often refers to as the real soul of the winery, is understandably one of the people he is most thankful for. His brother-in-law, Louis, provides unquestioning support, which is only possible from someone who shares and believes in the power of dreams. Len is often heard saying, "We sell wine, but what we really sell is the permission to dream big." True to his testament that if you dream it, you can achieve it, The Foreign Affair Winery was built on the Crispinos' passion and lust for life. The results of this binding together of two very different cultures to form a perfect blend—in life and wine—are undeniable.

Top and Bottom: The expansive, Italian-esque tasting room is both rustic and refined. Its stone fireplace and hearth epitomize warm, Old World appeal.

Middle: The winery's philosophy of "Sogni e Rinasci"—which means "dream and the world conspires"—is embossed on every cork.

Facing Page: Cyclists donning "fueled by wine" Foreign Affair jerseys pass the vineyards in an annual tour.
Photographs by Steven Elphick

Cabernet Franc
Superb with venison, wild boar, roast beef
with pan jus, or aged cheeses.

Cabernet Sauvignon
Ideal with steak, braised beef short ribs, or lamb ravioli.

Pinot Noir
Excellent with pork, pasta in fresh tomato sauces
with chicken bolognese, or mushroom risotto.

Riesling
Pair with canapés and hors d'oeuvres.

Tastings
Open to the public year-round,
appointments preferred for larger groups

Hernder Estate Wines

St. Catharines

Described as a "must see" destination winery, Hernder Estate Wines is known as much for aesthetical appeal as it is for award-winning vintages. A self-proclaimed wedding winery, the property is a rare find for brides and grooms the world over. Onsite ceremonies are conveniently paired with one of two elegant spaces for receptions that follow. Each room is complete with a cozy fireplace and romantic features, setting an intimate and relaxed tone for attendants to enjoy. The grounds are enchanting as well, home to a restored Victorian barn, circa 1867, and Niagara's only covered bridge. Built in 1995 for the celebration of Fred's first granddaughter, Brittany, the Brittany Bridge welcomes guests to discover and delight in the winery's many amenities.

Three generations of grape growers, dating back to 1939, have made Hernder what it is today. After Gottfried Hernder Sr. emigrated from Germany to Western Canada with his wife Helen, they settled on a farm of rich soil and vibrant assorted fruit. At 11 years old, Gottfried Jr.—referred to as Fred—left school with a 6th grade education and began working on his family's farm and meat shop to help out. This decision was key in developing the skills that would one day make him Niagara's youngest "Grape King." Today Fred, along with his wife Ricki, son Chris, and daughter Angel, all contribute to Hernder Estate and its overwhelming success.

Top: The estate produces a variety of VQA wines. From award-winning reds and whites to world-class icewines, the portfolio is impressive and diverse.

Middle: Owner Fred Hernder's vision of owning a winery in the 1980s is a reality today. Hernder Estate Wines has become a winery destination for many all over the world.

Bottom: Head winemaker Lydia Tomek holds a Bachelor of Science degree in enology and viticulture and is one of the youngest winemakers in her field.

Facing Page: Down a quiet country road, among the gentle swell of vineyards, and through a unique covered bridge sits the perfectly restored 1867 Victorian barn.
Photographs by Steven Elphick

In 2006, Lydia Tomek became head winemaker at Hernder, and with her a combined style of rustic tradition meets New World technology ensued. Specializing in riesling, icewine, and merlot, her addition was celebrated by the estate with a new label, noting her personal touch which is evident in all of the bottles. Her first release, Pink, is a dry rosé made from cabernet sauvignon and sauvignon blanc varietals. Blended to perfection, Pink was crafted for a saintly cause: The Hernder Picasso's Foundation. A nonprofit organization, the foundation donates proceeds from the specialty wine to the Regional Walker Cancer Centre.

Along with a number of other accolades, the winery has been granted the Sichel Trophy—an industry Emmy—for the best riesling in the world. As Lydia continues to put her heart and soul into each new creation, more acclaim is certain to follow.

Above: The tasting room is open year-round, seven days a week for wine sampling while touring the beautiful estate.

Left: A popular wedding venue, the rustic room boasts fireplaces, original beams, and stone walls that create the perfect ambience to entertain guests.

Facing Page: Floor-to-ceiling French and American oak barrels fill the room. It is a sight to behold and makes the perfect backdrop for photos.
Photographs by Steven Elphick

Vidal Icewine
Pair with honey-roasted pecans and Benedictine blue cheese.

Riesling
Pair with French kitchen fondue or citrus-glazed perch or pickerel.

Chardonnay
Pair with scallops in a chardonnay-based cream sauce.

Baco Noir
Pair with Southern barbecue or gourmet pizza.

Tastings
Open daily, year-round

HERNDER
ESTATE WINES

Kacaba
Vineyards & Winery

Vineland

Toronto Bay Street lawyer Michael Kacaba has Saskatchewan country roots. When he often traveled to Niagara with visitors in the early 1990s, he was surprised to see wine grapes being planted. Rather than dreaming about a move to Napa, he started researching and discovered that it was feasible for vinifera wines to survive winters in Niagara.

Michael knew location would be key. He found that the Niagara Escarpment Benches were being used for subdivisions rather than grapes, but that one prime lot of acreage in Vineland was not yet built out. Michael and his wife Joanne persevered and succeeded in buying it. It was a difficult plant that included leveling and terracing a ravine, but by 1998 grapes were growing there instead of vanity houses, all with a view of the Toronto skyline across Lake Ontario.

The Escarpment, the shoreline of prehistoric Lake Iroquois, drains air as well as frost, which is why when other areas freeze up in the fall grapes there are still green growing and have more hang time to develop concentrated flavors—in 2009, the last of Kacaba Vineyards & Winery's grapes were picked on November 23rd. Michael maintains that the cool climate produces wine with more flavor than hot deserts because grapes need phenolic maturity as well as sugar content. Bordeaux and Burgundy are at the same latitude as Niagara.

Top: Roses at the end of the vine rows act as sentinels; like the canary in the coal mine, they could signal a problem. Intense care of the vines has ensured that no alarm has ever been needed.
Photograph courtesy of Kacaba Vineyards & Winery

Middle: An elderly gentleman wanted the winery to have his antique basket press because he liked Kacaba wines. He wouldn't take money, but finally accepted some wine in exchange.
Photograph courtesy of Kacaba Vineyards & Winery

Bottom: While stabilization of ravine terraces is a challenge, hard work involved in planting, tending, and harvesting is a constant effort that yields premium grapes.
Photograph by Steven Elphick

Facing Page: Toronto's skyline across Lake Ontario is visible from the vineyard. Kacaba Vineyards is ecologically oriented and an originating member of Wine Council of Ontario Sustainability Group.
Photograph by Steven Elphick

Michael decided to plant only reds at his vineyard, including something new to Canada: syrah—his, and soon to be many others', favorite. There were no syrah vines in Canada, so he flew to Sonoma and brought back 29 crates of green growing vines as luggage, except for 11 the airline lost and detoured through Dallas.

Joanne and Michael continued working in Toronto, raising three daughters and attending to the multitude of things needed for their venture. They built a small winery on Lots 67 and 68 of the now defunct subdivision, started their 1999 vintage with contracted grapes, bought French oak barrels, and resolved to produce ultra-premium wines. The winery's signature ravine needed a bridge, eventually purchased from the St. Lawrence Seaway. The drive welcoming visitors needed trees, and after an extensive search, mature sugar maples were brought in and now blaze with color each fall. A gold medal and "Best Of" award for the couple's first wines eased their concerns.

Hang time and thinning, as well as hand-tending and harvesting, have paid off with regular major awards and medals. The 2007 cabernet sauvignon took gold at the 2010 Cuvée, a competition judged by winemakers, and then went on to score another gold medal at the Ontario Wine Awards. Notably, the 2007 syrah won Best Red in Canada in the 2009 Canadian Wine Awards,

Top: Awards from judges and winemakers verify that Kacaba Vineyards produces ultra-premium wines.
Photograph by Steven Elphick

Bottom: Joanne and Michael with daughters Susan, Jennifer, and Rebecca with sons-in-law Tim and Luke surveying grapes just before harvest.
Photograph by Alexander Anonychuk

Facing Page Top: In clay loam soil, vine roots over 50 feet deep take up water-soluble minerals, resulting in unique flavors that express the terroir.
Photograph courtesy of Kacaba Vineyards & Winery

Facing Page Bottom: The Lieutenant Governor of Ontario, The Honourable David C. Onley, and foreign diplomats have visited Kacaba Vineyards, recognizing the winery's 2012 award for excellence in Ontario wines.
Photograph ©stecphoto.com

marking the first time an Ontario winery had taken Best Red in this competition. Winemaker John Tummon's lifelong career in vinification and judging has proven invaluable in crafting exceptional grapes into ultra-premium wine.

At Kacaba, it is often hard to repeat a purchase, as releases regularly sell out. A loyal customer base knows to pre-order and stock up by the case. Kacaba regularly holds back sales until its premium wines have had a chance to age and develop further. Its 2002 releases, which on young vines developed stellar flavors and complexity over the years, are now rare.

A small and intimate tasting room is carved out of the production winery, Victorian-inspired and clad in board and batten. Customers frequently note that retail manager Dave Servos and his staff are friendly and excited about introducing their wines, conducting impromptu or pre-arranged tours and tastings, and recommending other wineries and destinations. The winery is often jammed full with exuberant visitors sipping, discussing, and learning more about wine.

Top: Local Vietnamese workers prune each vine during winter, tuck shoots, pull leaves, thin the crop during summer, and harvest in late fall—all carefully and patiently by hand.
Photograph courtesy of Kacaba Vineyards & Winery

Middle Left: Joanne and Michael in the tank room—missing their straw hats and hayforks.
Photograph by Steven Elphick

Middle Right: Cycling visitors from one of Niagara's many trails are often seen at Kacaba Vineyards, although it is not the easiest way to transport wine.
Photograph by Steven Elphick

Bottom: The bistro plays host to a variety of private functions. Local foods, specialties, flowers, and entertainment are offered, thus supporting neighbors.
Photograph courtesy of Kacaba Vineyards & Winery

Facing Page Top: Summer plantings at the bistro and winery are an expression of another agricultural activity especially suited to Niagara and have been noted for special recognition.
Photograph by Steven Elphick

Facing Page Bottom: Sleeping grapes exemplify cold climate viticulture. The Bailey Bridge—of movie fame—stretches over the lower portion of the ravine.
Photograph courtesy of Kacaba Vineyards & Winery

Joanne and Michael's daughters worked at the winery and, although they have since embarked on their own professional careers and families, are never far from the progress at this family-oriented enterprise. Their names are often used on the non-varietals, such as Jennifer's Jade Icewine, Rebecca Rosé, and Susie's Select Late Harvest. Family and patron Christmas parties are special, because harvest has just finished and the winery and crush pad get a good clean up and an influx of visitors. Most events are held in a beveled glass-enclosed patio and bistro, where decorations, a profusion of lights, and a small herd of wire reindeer all add up to a festive atmosphere.

Going forward, and with LCBO stores' initiatives in mind, Kacaba has released moderately priced blends that had previously only been available at the winery from time to time: Gypsy Red and Gypsy White. These have enjoyed a resounding success. Kacaba is following up with a release of a new blend—iWine—that speaks to a more tech-savvy clientele through technological means on the label and with current tastes tending to rich and fruit-forward.

Kacaba prides itself on its record of sustainable agricultural and winemaking practices and continues its mission of producing vvv premium wines. After all, when Michael was considering names for the winery, he was told to put his own name on it if he intended to assure his customers that he stands behind the value and quality of his product.

Top: The retail shop is decorated with a painting of boats at anchor on a hot day. The image is featured on Kacaba Vineyards' Rebecca Rosé label.

Bottom: The winery is tucked in between grapevines and natural features of the Niagara Escarpment.

Facing Page: Canadian sugar maples in fall colors lead up the driveway to the bridge and ravine, but the grapevines are still green, their fruit maturing for full flavor.
Photographs by Steven Elphick

Reserve Syrah
Delicious with slow-roasted venison drizzled
with a wine-and-blackberry reduction.

Reserve Cabernet Franc
Pairs well with grilled leg of lamb served
with spiced mustard and rosemary.

Reserve Meritage
Serve alongside Southwest blackened beef ribeye.

Reserve Cabernet Sauvignon
Delicious with porcini-crusted beef tenderloin.

Tastings
Open to the public year-round

KACABA
VINEYARDS & WINERY

Le Clos Jordanne

Jordan Station

When Jean-Charles Boisset first came to the Niagara Escarpment, he claims he could feel a certain je ne sais quoi about the region's terroir. A Burgundy wine producer from France, Jean-Charles was interested in Niagara's land due to its growing reputation and choice climate. Resembling the Côte d'Or—site of the celebrated vineyards in Burgundy, France—the Escarpment revealed a variety of minerals in the soil as well as changes in elevation. Working closely with the estate's original winemaker and viticulturist, Thomas Bachelder, Jean-Charles discovered vineyard locations in Jordan with plantings of pinot noir and chardonnay grapes worthy of this international investment.

Spanning the Escarpment slope in Jordan, four vineyards—totaling more than 132 acres—contribute fruit to the label. The one-time shoreline of ancient Lake Iroquois, the Escarpment was formed by glaciers carrying sandstone, limestone, and dolomites rich in loam, clay, sand, gravel, and other minerals during the last Ice Age. The varying nutrients, combined with changing elevation in the slope, make for endless options and an assortment of lots. Applying a Burgundian practice of mixing clones within planting blocks, the estate focuses on the effects of the terroir and tightly spaces the vines, ensuring well colonized land with lower yields but prime results due to wider access to nutrients and sunlight.

The estate's grapes are cared for by hand from vine to wine. From pruning to shoot-thinning and positioning to leaf plucking and harvesting, gentle hands do the job. Additionally, synthetic fertilizers, fungicides, pesticides, or herbicides are never applied, as the workers are stewards of the vines that honor their sense of place.

Top: Le Clos Jordanne champions classic single vineyards for cool-climate chardonnay and pinot noir.

Bottom: Chardonnay and pinot noir quietly age in French oak, all the while absorbing character from the barrels.

Facing Page: Water cascades over Niagara Escarpment rock at Ball's Falls in Jordan.
Photographs by Steven Elphick

Among the stewards are winemaker Sébastien Jacquey and vineyard manager Gerald Klose, whose close work ensures the legacy of previous vintages will carry on. Sébastien's dynamic, patient, and diligent approach to winemaking is enhanced by his rigorous training, internship, and apprentice experience. A private tasting in Niagara redirected Sébastien's path in 2007. A tourist to the country, he had only met Thomas Bachelder—then winemaker—once before in Burgundy for an interview. Still unsure about the move to Ontario, Sébastien was invited by Thomas to a blind tasting. Especially gifted with pinot noir, Sébastien confused a Burgundy wine from Chambolle-Musigny, an actual village in Burgundy, with one from Le Clos Jordanne. Thus convinced of Niagara's potential to craft

a superior and elegant pinot noir, he journeyed across the world to do just that. Educated in the finest French institutions, such as Baron Philippe de Rothschild in Pauillac, Sébastien has a master's degree of earth and environment, specializing in vine management and terroir along with an engineering degree in enology and viticulture. Past positions at châteaux in the Nevers region of Burgundy via Dijon, the Loire Valley, Corsica, and Bordeaux all contribute to the practical knowledge he has acquired.

Above: Nestled atop the Claystone Terrace Vineyard in the Twenty Mile Bench sub-appellation, golden-toned pinot noir vines relax after a harvest.

Right: Ripened pinot noir clusters are ready for harvest.

Facing Page: Individual blocks mark plantings from 2001, identifying specific clones and root stocks in Le Clos Jordanne's vineyard.
Photographs by Steven Elphick

Winner of the highly coveted Judgment of Montreal—a blind tasting held in Quebec for *Cellier* magazine—a 2005 Claystone Terrace Chardonnay put Le Clos Jordanne on the map and caused an international coup. The bottle was a wild-card wine, competing against industry titans from France and California. Its unexpected win has since made Canada an esteemed source of viniferous wines and Le Clos Jordanne a worldwide icon.

The estate became part of Constellation Brands in 2006 through the purchase of Vincor International. Since that time, wines continue to be described by enthusiasts as stunning, astounding, majestic, brilliant, sophisticated, elegant, and spectacular. Perhaps Richard Sands summed it up best in *Wine Business International*: "Le Clos Jordanne is producing pinot noir that is as great as any in the world."

Top: Wines mature in French oak barrels from Sirugue, Cadus, Damy, Marsannay, Chassin, Billon, Berthomieu, Rousseau, and Mercurey for a minimum of 15 months.

Bottom: Sébastien Jacquey brings a passion for chardonnay and pinot noir to Le Clos Jordanne's signature winemaking style.

Facing Page: The barrel room is a place of patience, where time-honored traditions slowly reach fruition when becoming fine wines.
Photographs by Steven Elphick

Le Clos Jordanne Vineyard Chardonnay
Pair with cauliflower gratin.

Village Reserve Pinot Noir
Pair with beet and quinoa salad with pinot noir vinaigrette.

Village Reserve Chardonnay
Pair with parsnip soup.

Le Clos Jordanne Vineyard Pinot Noir
Pair with truffled white beans.

Tastings
Closed to the public

LE CLOS JORDANNE™

Megalomaniac Wines

Vineland

A truly original approach to deliver quality above all else, Megalomaniac Wines reflects the integration of land, climate, and people. This results in cleverly packaged and deeply decadent wines that shrug off pretention and encourage spirited attention. Proprietor John Howard named his winery Megalomaniac after close friends laughingly dismissed his original idea: a winery named after himself. Accusing him of being some kind of megalomaniac—a person with an inflated sense of self-esteem and overestimation—the name stayed and John embraces it in several ways. Cringing at the somewhat high-brow stereotype that wineries, critics, and winemakers seem to exude, John light-heartedly plays up the narcissistic image and grandiose position by donning an email address of ego@megalomaniacwine.com and keeping the quote "conceit is thinking you're great; egotism is knowing it" on the website. Fittingly, his portfolio of wines bears witty names and clever descriptions resulting in best-selling, award-winning vintages that impress even the haughtiest aficionados.

Resident enologist Sue-Ann Staff is the magic behind the magnificent vintages at Megalomaniac. Meant to be shared with friends of equivalent or even greater egos, these wines are perfectly paired with delusional fantasies of wealth, power, and occasional omnipotence, according to the brand. Bigmouth and Bravado are just a couple of the brazenly titled wines available. Described as defiant, gutsy, and self-assured, Bravado is a proud cabernet sauvignon while Bigmouth is said to be a powerful merlot; neither timid nor a wallflower. On the lighter side, rieslings such as Homegrown and Narcissist, along with Coldhearted riesling icewine, present wine enthusiasts with precocious choices as well.

Top and Bottom: The doors and hardware were executed by local artisans.

Facing Page: John Howard's residence has been dubbed by locals as Castle Howard, although its actual title is The Home Vineyard.
Photographs by Steven Elphick

Megalomaniac began as a retirement project for John, the former proprietor of Vineland Estates Winery. He kept 100 acres of land for farming after its sale and planted European grape vines in 1995. Creating the first vintage for a worthy cause—a foundation to aid long-term care or terminally ill children—John donated proceeds to Kids' Health Links, which allows children to connect to family, friends, and school with laptop computers. He continues to give a portion of the winery's earnings to the cause, a percentage of the estimated 20,000 cases he produces each year.

Above: The 96-acre Sous Terre Vineyard is owned and operated by Megalomaniac proprietor John Howard, and it provides merlot, cabernet sauvignon, cabernet franc, pinot noir, and riesling for the illustrious brand.

Right: The fermentation room was custom-designed and manufactured by Jean-Louis Mangeard of Jarnac, France.

Facing Page: Beyond the front entrance, a 12,000-square-foot underground cellar houses an impressive collection of estate wines. *Photographs by Steven Elphick*

An avid lover of the French culture, as evidenced by a degree in French and fine art, John is influenced by the Old World European charm of the Bordeaux wine-producing region. As part owner of Chateau La Confession and Chateau Haut Pontet in Saint-Émilion, France, he understands, perhaps more than most, the passion necessary to produce internationally respected Bordeaux varietals.

Established in 2007, the vineyard is owned and operated by John, and is filled with varietals imported from France as well as a riesling from the Mosel Valley in Germany. Reflective of a medieval setting, the underground cellar spans 12,000 square feet of thick stone submerged beneath the ground. The site is marked by an awe-inspiring archway encompassed by stone walls, divided by epic iron gates. A small-scale French château, with castle-like influences, sits adjacent to the Megalomaniac property, completing the Old World fantasy.

Perched atop the highest point of the Niagara Escarpment, the property enjoys views of the majestic Niagara Falls, serene Lake Ontario, and towering cityscape of Toronto. Patrons can peruse the grounds or journey below the surface for a wine cave discovery.

Top: The home vineyard's private tasting room is ornately dressed in rich textiles and formal furnishings.

Middle: A private cellar at Castle Howard is an intimate space for exclusive entertainment.

Bottom: Estate proprietor John Howard.

Facing Page: The barrel room and cellar are located just below the Sous Terre Vineyard.
Photographs by Steven Elphick

Narcissist Riesling
Pair with maple-smoked salmon and wild rice.

Bigmouth Merlot
Pair with foie gras and garlic-roasted potatoes.

SOB Pinot Noir
Pair with Mandarin orange-marinated duck and seasoned vegetables.

Tastings
Open to the public daily

Mike Weir Winery

Beamsville

Everyone loves to root for the underdog. In both professional golf and the wine industry, Mike Weir was initially underestimated. But, like the Ontario wine country, Mike has surpassed all expectations to become an icon.

Mike became a household name to golf fans after his 2003 Masters Tournament championship, which made him the first Canadian male to win a major professional golf title. Along the way, Mike was seen as the underdog on the golf circuit. Despite his small stature, being left-handed, and not having access to the top coaches, Mike made it to the PGA Tour with undeniable determination and focus, all of which he still maintains alongside his second profession: fine wine. Soon after his Masters win, Mike and his wife Bricia decided to turn their love of wine into a business. The result was Mike Weir Winery, established in 2005.

Likening wine to a journey, Mike went from a childhood of making wine with his Italian grandfather in Niagara Falls—with a successful detour on the golf course—into the Ontario wine industry. Was it his underdog status in golf that prompted him to establish his winery? Perhaps, but the larger impetus was grounded in his love of wine and the birth of the Mike Weir Foundation in 2004, which helps children with physical, mental, and financial needs. When the idea to build a wine business came up, Mike knew it would be a great opportunity to support the foundation, which has donated millions of dollars to various hospitals and nonprofit organizations for research and treatment. All profits from the winery go to the Mike Weir Foundation. Mike believes that if his success in golf and the wine industry can help children, then that is worth far more than any green jacket or accolades he could receive.

Top: Mike Weir enjoying a glass of cabernet merlot in his vineyard.

Bottom: Grapes gently warm in the Ontario sunshine.

Facing Page: The vineyards of Mike Weir Winery sit in the heart of the Beamsville Bench.
Photographs by Steven Elphick

Mike Weir produces an array of wines, including chardonnay, cabernet merlot, sauvignon blanc, pinot noir, riesling, rosé, sparkling wine, and icewine. Under its Underdog Wine Co. label, the winery produces a red and a white blend. Premium reserve wines are also available for purchase in very limited quantities at the winery only. As the Underdog Wine bottles state, Mike Weir wine wants to stand out from the rest. It's not only committed to charity and disproving assumptions about the underdog, but is also a family-oriented business. Mike's brother Jim Weir serves as CEO, Mike's wife Bricia takes an active design role, and family recipes are shared with patrons for food and wine pairings.

Right: Mike's determination, passion, and focus are captured in the Underdog label design.

Facing Page Top: Mike chooses a vintage chardonnay from the Weir wine library cellar.

Facing Page Bottom Left: In wine, as in golf, passion plays a strong role in the delivery of the best result.

Facing Page Bottom Right: French oak barrels are used to age the cabernet merlot and pinot noir.
Photographs by Steven Elphick

The hospitality center at Mike Weir Winery greets guests with a Tuscan-style warmth that mirrors Mike and Bricia's home in Utah, as well as sweeping views of the vineyards, Lake Ontario, and downtown Toronto. From the vaulted ceilings to the large welcoming fireplace, the center's purpose is to provide guests with room to converse, relax, and enjoy their favorite Mike Weir wines. The three-story building features a demonstration kitchen in which visiting chefs toss fresh ingredients and wow visitors with their signature fare. The third story houses a gallery of memorabilia from Mike's golf career and also serves as a private tasting room. In the future, Mike and his team hope to make various parts of the property available for charity and fundraising events to further help children in need.

Above: Mike Weir Winery offers an array of VQA vinifera wines.

Left: Mike enjoys tasting his favorite chardonnay.

Facing Page: One of the finest views of Lake Ontario and Toronto may be had atop the sloping vineyards of Mike Weir Winery.
Photographs by Steven Elphick

Pinot Noir
Perfect with grilled salmon, lamb, and pork, and medium-aged cheeses.

Chardonnay
Pairs well with roast poultry, pork, or cream-based pastas.

Cabernet Merlot
Delicious with beef, lamb, duck, and aged cheeses.

Tastings
Open to the public daily, year-round

MIKE WEIR WINERY

Puddicombe Estate
Farms & Winery

Winona

Situated on 130 prime acres on Ontario's sub-appellation Lincoln Lakeshore, Puddicombe Estate Farms & Winery stands as a contradiction to impersonal production and lost traditions. On this temperate lakeshore, buildings are constructed from 100-year-old barn beams, wines are given all the time they need to mature, and generations of Puddicombes work together to preserve the spirit of independent viticulture.

This seventh-generation farm, deeded to the family in 1797 by King George III, enjoys the rare distinction of not only being the first winery on the Niagara Wine Route but also of sitting on a prime, fertile strip between Lake Ontario and the Niagara Escarpment. Here, thanks to favorable thermal conditions, lake breezes bring warm air in the winter and chase away heat and humidity in the summer. The resulting climate is magical for viticulture and has resulted in Puddicombe's award-winning selections of aromatic, fruit-driven reds and fresh, bright whites.

Notably laid-back and cooperative, the farm is a wonderland of meticulously tended arbors, rough-timbered buildings, and over 200 acres of flowering fruit trees. The entire scene sings of agrarian charm and friendliness. Schoolchildren pet animals and learn about life on the farm, couples stop by for wine and dessert, and wines made from Puddicombe's exclusive Colombard grapes fly off the shelves.

Top: Puddicombe Estate is home to a regional rarity, a Colombard white wine, while Summerville Pinot Rosé is a much-loved member of the Pinot Noir Trio.

Bottom: A mural on wooden planks depicts the estate's Little Pud train, which gives agricultural tours around the property.

Facing Page: The serene pond is lined with 50-something-year-old willow trees and an abundance of wildlife.
Photographs by Steven Elphick

Most notable—and featured on the winery's label—is the Puddicombe train, a one-of-a-kind attraction that transports guests on a host of different tours around the property, from 25-minute sipping rides to "taste of viticulture" tours with four fruit-sampling stops along the way to culinary tours, where courses are served at stops along the route and guests regroup for wine and dessert back in the timbered bar.

The farm's transition into a winery grew out of a friendship between Stoney Ridge vintner Jim Warren and seventh-generation owner Murray Puddicombe. Jim had been sourcing grapes from Murray since he started making wine in his garage. The two joined forces and developed Stoney Ridge wines on the Puddicombe farm until the late 1990s, when the two parted ways.

Operating under the philosophy that a farm should reflect the character of its owners, Murray and his wife Carolyn—who took over operations from Murray's father, just as their daughter Lindsay and son Brock will assume stewardship after them—shunned the idea of elite tastings and exclusivity in favor of farm-style friendliness and come-one-come-all hospitality. Today families drive from as far as 100 miles away to fill their trunks with Puddicombe's pick-your-own cherries, apples, pears, and pumpkins.

Above: A rustic barn, original to the property, flanks the estate marketplace with a winery, café, and bakery inside.

Right: Choco is the estate's pet donkey and a valuable member of the petting farm.

Facing Page: The pristine Niagara Escarpment is captured from many vantage points on the grounds.
Photographs by Steven Elphick

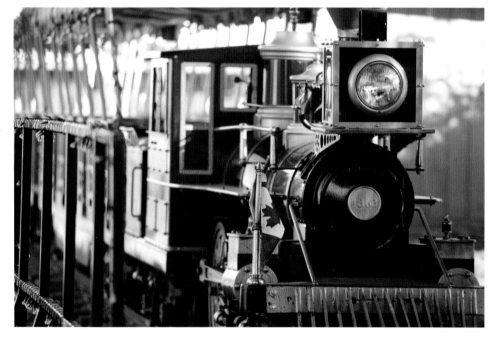

Inside the farm store, pints of peaches, plums, grapes, blueberries, and raspberries round out the selection while bottles of Puddicombe's pinot noir, seyval blanc, and award-winning icewines make cellar-worthy mementos.

Tradition of stewardship shows no sign of flagging. The next generation is in place and poised for the transition. Head winemaker Lindsay Puddicombe, a certified enologist, has already won awards for her wines and been nominated for the Premier's Award for Excellence in Winemaking. Her brother Brock studied western agriculture before spending six months working and studying at a vineyard in New Zealand. The mileage paid off when he developed his Sir Isaac Pear Cider, made from 100-percent Niagara-grown pears. The cider, which is a resounding success, also helps the community by giving local farmers an outlet for their surplus pear crops.

Maintaining an independent farm in the middle of an urban society is never easy. Corporate competition and local regulations compound the normal challenges of growing fruit and doing business. But as large numbers of young winemakers like Lindsay and Brock bring new life and sustainable practices to the industry, the opportunity for responsible growth will remain strong. This bodes well, because for Murray, Carolyn, Lindsay, and Brock Puddicombe, educating wine lovers, conveying their love of the land, and creating exceptional wines remains their undisputed family mission.

Top: The Puddicombe family: Brock, Carolyn, Murray, and Lindsay invite guests to enjoy the beautiful farm and charming winery by foot or by train.

Middle: The Little Pud offers agricultural train rides, culinary tours, and tasting adventures.

Bottom and Facing Page: Inside the tasting room and retail store, visitors encounter a number of nationally and internationally recognized wines and award-winning vintages to sample and take home to share.
Photographs by Steven Elphick

Puddicombe Cabernet Franc Icewine
Perfect with Bosc pears grilled with apricot jam and honey.

Puddicombe Pinot Noir
Pair with bacon and horseradish-stuffed roast beef
with a pinot noir reduction.

Puddicombe Gamay Noir
Delicious alongside grilled minted lamb chops.

Tastings
Open to the public daily, year round

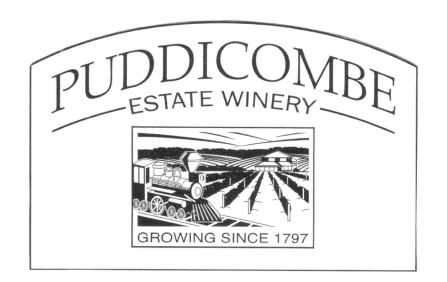

GROWING SINCE 1797

Royal DeMaria
Canada's Icewine Specialists

Beamsville

Anytime Her Majesty Queen Elizabeth and Sir Richard Branson share an interest, the coincidence is worth noting. In this case, the passion is not for falconry or military strategy, but the superior icewines produced by Royal DeMaria Canada's Icewine Specialists™. The winery was graced with a request from Her Majesty Queen Elizabeth during the Queen's Jubilee visit to Canada in 2002. Sir Richard Branson has also visited the winery, in 2003, and he purchased six bottles.

In 1994, four years before he would present his first icewine to the public, Joseph DeMaria knew that he wanted to specialize exclusively in the production of icewine and immediately worked to be the best in the industry. While it may seem bullish to dub oneself a specialist before there is a wine market—or even a facility—Joseph's confidence in his ability to perfect the form ended up being a self-fulfilling prophecy. In 1998, he began fermenting his first icewine from a 5,000 liter surplus of vidal icewine juice. However, midway through the process, Joseph made an undisclosed yet potentially batch-killing error. He countered with a blind correction, and in doing so, happened upon a new winemaking technique. The novice correction produced a product with all the varietal characteristics of fine wine and the traditional sweetness of an icewine, yet without the cloying finish. The Royal DeMaria 1998 Vidal Icewine went on to win five international awards and the "error" has been the winemaking technique that Joseph has used successfully ever since.

Top: Snow covers the vines.

Bottom: Grapes for the icewines freeze on the vine.

Facing Page: The main building of Royal DeMaria Canada's Icewine Specialists™.
Photographs by Steven Elphick

Since that first vintage, the winery—with Joseph at the helm as president and winemaker—has gone on to produce the world's largest portfolio of icewines, 24 varietals of red and white to date, including the world's first Meritage Icewine 2002, the world's most expensive icewine, Royal DeMaria 2000 Chardonnay Icewine, and an impressive array from gewürztraminer icewine to Muscat icewine and pinot noir icewines. Joseph has internationally trademarked Royal DeMaria Wines "Canada's Icewine Specialists" and Royal DeMaria Wines is the only winery in the world to specialize exclusively in the production of icewine.

Royal DeMaria wines are recognized as being among the world's finest. Joseph has brought home eight world wine records, including five prestigious Citadelles du Vin gold trophies, France 2002, five consecutive gold medals from Chardonnay du Monde, France 2005-2009, five gold medals Concours Mondial, Belgium 2003, seven trophies in the icewine category Citadelles du Vin France 2006, and nine double-gold medals from Finger Lakes International Wine Competition USA 2000-2009. The riesling icewine was served at the 2008 G8 Summit in Hokkaido, Japan, and bottles of the Royal DeMaria 2008 Cabernet Franc Icewine were purchased by the Canadian government and given as gifts to the G 20 leaders during the 2010 G 20 Summit in Toronto.

Right: A bottle of the highly prized Royal DeMaria icewine.

Facing Page Top: Awards line the walls of the tasting room.

Facing Page Bottom: Royal DeMaria icewines are recognized as among the best in the world.
Photographs by Steven Elphick

This international recognition has vaulted a number of DeMaria's wines to collectible status. To satisfy the needs of his most ardent collectors, Joseph designated a Collector's Series that includes icewines that are no longer available in commercial volumes. Collectors gladly pay $3,500 for a bottle of that initial, remarkable 1998 Vidal Icewine and up to $18,000 for a bottle of the landmark 2002 Meritage Icewine.

The Royal DeMaria 2000 Chardonnay Icewine, the first to be entered into the highly prestigious and exclusive Billy Myers Series, has garnered international recognition to include the patronage of a Saudi businessman who paid $30,000 for a bottle in New York City in 2006. The final bottle of this fine icewine will be sold for $500,000. Since its initial release, it has won gold for five consecutive years at the coveted Chardonnay-du-Monde in Chaintré, France, and five consecutive titles at the prestigious Les Citadelles du Vin Vinexpo in Bordeaux, France.

Royal DeMaria icewines are so well known and highly valued that they have received extraordinary prices in international charity auctions, namely: Royal DeMaria 2002 Meritage Icewine received $8,000 per bottle in Connecticut, 2007, $7,738 per bottle in Hong Kong, 2010, and $11,000 per bottle in Hong Kong 2011.

Above: A collection of Royal DeMaria icewines.

Facing Page: The vines at harvest time.
Photographs by Steven Elphick

Icewine

Pairs well with foie gras, sharp cheese, and fresh fruit.
Flawless with spicy Thai or Indian cuisine.

Tastings

Open to the public daily, year-round by appointment or by chance

ROYAL
DeMARIA

'CANADA'S ICEWINE SPECIALISTS'

Stoney Ridge
Estate Winery

Vineland

Fluttering butterflies, willows swaying in the wind, and trickling waterfalls. These are the sights and sounds one might expect in a luxurious botanical garden, but when visitors arrive at Stoney Ridge Estate Winery, they're overcome by the same wonders. Known for its award-winning gardens as well as its award-winning wines, Stoney Ridge has experienced a metamorphosis that mirrors the butterflies that dance among its flowering grapevines.

Stoney Ridge opened in July of 1985 with a spirited commitment to producing small amounts of the best wine possible, using only Ontario grapes. Migrating from its original location in Stoney Creek to its current home of Vineland in the Niagara Escarpment, Stoney Ridge has gone from producing just 4,000 cases annually in its first years to being one of the premier wineries in Ontario. Over the years, the Stoney Ridge name has become synonymous with exceptional quality, innovation, and a flare for the exotic. As an Ontario wine innovator, Stoney Ridge created Canada's first unoaked chardonnay and garnered praise for its much sought-after cranberry fruit wine. By 1997, Stoney Ridge had amassed more awards than any other Canadian winery.

Today Stoney Ridge continues to produce one of Niagara's most extensive portfolios of white and red wines, icewines, fruit wines, and other unique delights. It is Stoney Ridge's chardonnays and pinot noirs, however, that are the foundation of its success. The 2009 Excellence Chardonnay received gold at the 2012 Cuvée Awards, as well as the 2011 Lieutenant Governor of Ontario Award of Excellence. As if to further illustrate this point,

Top: Aptly named, Stoney Ridge's Excellence Chardonnay and Excellence Pinot Noir have captured multiple prestigious awards.
Photograph by Steven Elphick

Bottom: Nestled within the Japanese shade garden, the trickling stone waterfall offers a tranquil retreat to winery visitors.
Photograph by Marion Adams

Facing Page: The Stoney Ridge wine boutique charms visitors with its friendly, casual feel. Two tasting bars welcome visitors to find their favorite wine.
Photograph by Steven Elphick

the 2010 Excellence Chardonnay followed suit, capturing a double gold at the 2012 All-Canadian Wine Championships and a repeat win at the 2012 Lieutenant Governor Awards. The pinot noirs have similarly amassed rave reviews with an Intervin Best Value award for 2010 Warren Classic Pinot Noir and double gold kudos for 2009 Excellence Pinot Noir at the 2011 All-Canadian Wine Championships.

Yet even with so many awards and accolades, Stoney Ridge retains a friendly, warm atmosphere. The former farmhouse has been converted into a charming retail store and wine tasting bar. The artisan cheese boutique offers an array of local and international cheeses, including such novelties as mango-ginger Stilton, caramelized onion Cheddar, and even chocolate cheese. Visitors may enjoy a picnic at the winery with a stroll through the Japanese shade garden and a delectable Winemakers Basket lunch among the trailing roses of the lush garden patio.

Top: Guests may indulge in a moment of quiet contemplation amongst the colorful blooms.
Photograph by Marion Adams

Middle Left: The artisan cheese boutique features a delectable selection of local and international cheese for the perfect wine pairing.
Photograph courtesy of Stoney Ridge Estate Winery

Middle Right: Often called "a hidden gem," the exquisite gardens at Stoney Ridge welcome visitors with many delightful surprises.
Photograph by Marion Adams

Bottom: The warm, oaky atmosphere of the barrel room holds the secrets to exceptional winemaking.
Photograph courtesy of Stoney Ridge Estate Winery

Facing Page: The spectacular 75-foot rose-covered trellis offers the perfect spot to enjoy a glass of wine and light lunch.
Photograph by Steven Elphick

WINE & FARE

Excellence Chardonnay
Pairs exquisitely with lobster ravioli in vanilla butter sauce.

Excellence Pinot Noir
Perfect with wild mushroom risotto.

Cranberry Wine
Delicious with turkey Waldorf sandwich.

Sauvignon Blanc
Excellent with frisée and baby greens salad
with grapefruit-citrus vinaigrette.

Tastings
Open to the public daily, year-round

Sue-Ann Staff
Estate Winery

Jordan

As one of the oldest producing vineyards in Canada, Sue-Ann Staff Estate Winery is a living legacy. The first vines were planted in 1898 by proprietor Sue-Ann Staff's great-great-grandfather, Elisha Staff, and Sue-Ann's great-great-uncle. These vines are still present today and are an important part of the estate's 104 acres on the Niagara Escarpment.

Sue-Ann is a fifth-generation grape grower. A visionary, she has been instrumental in transforming the family business into a world-renowned winery. In 2002, she received the prestigious winemaker of the year award from The Ontario Wine Society. She has also been recognized twice as one of the world's top four women in wine during the highly acclaimed International Wine and Spirits competition in London, England.

Visiting the winery is a personal and intimate experience. People walk onto the grounds, where Sue-Ann's parents, brother, and sister-in-law also work, and are able to pet Sue-Ann's dog Brix and taste wine in her kitchen in the renovated 120-year-old farmstead home. The winery is an invitation to be treated like family and take part in the Staffs' celebration of life. Sue-Ann offers formal dining events in her home, hiring private chefs to prepare the cuisine while she casually discusses wines and pairings with guests. In addition to tours, tastings, and conversation, visitors get to catch a glimpse of a very unique asset: a pair of grass landing strips that officially make the estate the only fly-in winery in Niagara. Appropriately, all of the family members can pilot a plane.

Top: The Staff family homestead, built in 1883, houses a tasting room, retail store, and private dining quarters. A complete renovation in 2006 ensures historical features will be preserved for generations to come.

Bottom: Inspired by the red seal adorning the wine labels, a large red "S" constructed by Sue-Ann's father, Howard, marks the winery from the roadside.

Facing Page: Cabernet franc vines flank one of two grass landing strips in the vineyard. A family of avid pilots, the Staffs accommodate visitors by air.
Photographs by Steven Elphick

Sue-Ann used to refer to the winery as a modern winery, but during a visit from an Australian university friend, her friend joked that they had "lost her to the French." Sue-Ann admits that Old World techniques have crept into her New World winemaking. Perhaps this is due to her exposure to the French techniques of winemaking during her two annual trips to Saint-Émilion, the oldest wine area in the Bordeaux region in France. There, she liaises with Château La Confession Winery, coincidentally owned by Ontario's Megalomaniac Wines, where Sue-Ann is a consulting winemaker.

The family's flagship wine is riesling, which is grown classically on clay soil to help preserve the fruit's acidity, brightness, and citrus quality. Sue-Ann likens her riesling to the riesling produced in the Mosel Valley in Germany.

Releasing about 2,000 cases of lovingly crafted wine each year, Sue-Ann Staff Estate Winery's dedicated team absolutely lives and breathes winemaking, and the authenticity of their wines is palpable in the first sip.

Top: Proprietor and winemaker Sue-Ann enjoys sharing her life's passion with visitors daily.

Middle: Sitting in the front of the farmhouse, a traditional parlor dressed in gold and antiqued tones has been preserved in 1880s styles.

Bottom: A contemporary kitchen serves as a tasting room for guests to try one of Sue-Ann's fine wines.

Facing Page: Set for silver service, the ornate French-inspired dining room is prepped for five-course dinners courtesy of a professional chef.
Photographs by Steven Elphick

WINE & FARE

Pinot Grigio
Ideal with fish, chicken, poultry, pork, and mild to medium-bodied hard cheeses.

Robert's Block Riesling
Pair with chicken, poultry, seafood, and mild cheese.

Baco Noir
Serve with grilled meats and veggies, ratatouille, burgers, pastas, pâté, and dark chocolate.

Tastings
Open to the public daily, year-round

SUE-ANN
STAFF
ESTATE WINERY

Tawse Winery

Vineland

As a youth, Moray Tawse was extremely fascinated by the history of wine and the exciting, far-away places that it would come from. Drawn to its exotic origin, it became his first beverage of choice at a youngish age, which accounts for his diverse palate and aficionado ranking. After researching the potential for winemaking and good terroir in Niagara, he purchased his first vineyard in 2001 on the famed and protected Niagara Escarpment and opened Tawse Winery, a showcase six-level, gravity-fed winery, just four years later. Moray's mission to create wines of singular distinction from unique terroir plots, while conserving the earth's precious resources in the process, has influenced Ontario and its expanding wine industry. By doing so, he has fortified a new standard of farming practice in agribusiness, producing an impeccable and highly sought-after product without compromising the integrity of the land, animals, or habitat it was sourced from.

Living out the philosophy that great wine begins in the vineyard, Moray uses organic and biodynamic farming methods—a practice that recognizes the earth as a single, self-regulating, multi-dimensional ecosystem—which account for strong, pure, and more vibrant fruit to display the unique terroir of each lot. Beneath the rows and rows of grapevines exists the soil, which he believes is a living organism in its own right due to the shared work of flora and fauna. Flora—plant life—and fauna—insects, spiders, and predatory mites—act in tandem within the vineyard's ecosystem, thereby creating a self-sustaining entity capable of surviving without the assistance of manmade, destructive products.

Top: Inviting the public to visit, the winery's sign at the street is a massive slab of natural granite.

Bottom and Facing Page: The property is dotted with sculpture and fountains, while manicured gardens accentuate the ornate pieces.
Photographs by Steven Elphick

Because biodynamic wines are not usually produced on a large scale, business owners speculate that they are not as profitable as traditional viticulture. In contrast, Moray believes that when people are good to the earth, it returns the sentiment and produces fruit of matchless flavor and aromas, something that consumers are sure to recognize. Over time, revitalizing the earth and creating wines that are truly pure, in both spirit and consistency, is well worth the investment. The benefits of their holistic approach include divine balance, exceptional flavor, and recognizable aromas produced without harmful chemicals for diligent consumers.

Concerned with the environmental effects that agribusiness everywhere is responsible for, Moray hopes that gentle organic and biodynamic methods for biodiversity, soil fertility, crop nutrition, as well as pest, weed, and disease control, will catch on throughout the industry. The benefits of creating a self-contained vineyard would advantage both farmers and consumers while preventing further destruction of vital resources. Damaging pesticides, fungicides, and chemical fertilizers are replaced with natural predators and livestock—which also contribute to the soil's enrichment. A modern geothermal energy system furthers the estate's desire to minimize its environmental impact by reducing the use of traditional forms of energy by up to 80 percent. Additionally, a Wetland Biofilter facilitates the re-use of all sanitary and winery process water, minimizing water wasted. Bottles bearing seals by Ecocert and Demeter confirm that wines made by Tawse are genuinely eco-friendly, reinforcing the estate's saintly claim.

Left: Great wine starts in the vineyard. At Tawse, healthy, vibrant fruit that's organically grown and carefully hand-harvested is the key to exceptional wine.

Facing Page Top: Tawse Winery is nestled against the Niagara Escarpment on the Vineland Double Bench.

Facing Page Middle: A large pond and fountain create a magnificent foreground for the winery building.

Facing Page Bottom: The award-winning winery gardens surround the state-of-the-art facility.
Photographs by Steven Elphick

Releasing an initial vintage in 2001 with 200 cases of chardonnay and 200 cases of riesling, the winery, which began within the walls of an underdeveloped equipment barn, quickly became a boutique favorite. In 2005, the winery moved into a new facility constructed of local and regional materials, in continuance with the estate's carbon-conscious footprint. The production of varietals such as chardonnay, riesling, pinot noir, and cabernet franc have been perfected there, increasing the winery's success exponentially and even leading to it being named Canadian Winery of the Year by *Canadian Wine Access* magazine for two years consecutively.

An avid supporter of the Tawse philosophy, winemaker Paul Pender joined the team in 2005 and became head winemaker after just one year. Not only has he overseen the Ecocert organic and Demeter biodynamic certification process, he was named Winemaker of the

Year at the Ontario Wine Awards in 2011. Paul works in tandem with Pascal Marchand, a world-famous wine icon who gained renown during his tenure at Domaine des Epeneaux in Pommard, Burgundy. Known for his expertise in crafting terroir-based wines, Pascal consulted for a number of other wineries throughout the world, most notably in Burgundy, Chile, Australia, and California. Pascal's new ventures with Moray include Marchand-Tawse Negogiants in Nuit-Saint-Georges and Domaine Tawse in Beaune, France. Both of the new wineries are crafting vintages from over 35 exclusive vineyards in Burgundy.

Above Left: Owner Moray Tawse and winemaker Paul Pender in the barrel cellar.

Above Right: The Tawse name stands for quality and a dedication to the environment.

Facing Page: A selection of Tawse Winery's award-winning vintages.
Photographs by Steven Elphick

Six delicately cared-for vineyards make up the estate's supply of wholesome fruit: Cherry Avenue, Hillside, Quarry Road, Tintern Road, Limestone Ridge, and Redstone. Located within the Twenty Mile Bench sub-appellation of the Niagara Escarpment, Cherry Avenue nurtures some of the oldest vines of the area's chardonnay, riesling, pinot noir, merlot, and cabernet franc, divided into blocks bearing the names of Moray and his wife Joanne's three children. Consisting of chardonnay and pinot noir, Robyn's block cultivates highly admired varietals, while Carly's block grows some of the Niagara Escarpment's oldest riesling vines. The most expansive of the blocks belongs to David, featuring cabernet franc, merlot, chardonnay, and pinot noir. Just above the blocks, amazing views of neighboring Hillside plantings wait to be discovered. A vineyard consisting of cabernet sauvignon, chardonnay, pinot gris, and syrah

can be seen from many vantage points within Cherry Avenue's topography. Quarry Road is a short commute away, but well worth the drive. Situated on a slope scaling the Escarpment's rise in the Vinemont Ridge sub-appellation, varietals such as pinot noir, riesling, chardonnay, and gewürztraminer seem to cling to their high-altitude vines. Likewise pinot noir, exclusive to Tintern Road, shares the soaring elevation and unrivaled perspective. Descending back to sea level, Redstone stands alone in the Lincoln Lakeshore sub-appellation, with plantings of cabernet sauvignon, pinot gris, merlot,

Above: Lake Ontario provides important temperature moderation, essential for viticulture in the cool climate.

Right: Tawse is experimenting with tighter plantings—more vines per acre—to optimize quality.

Facing Page Bottom: Gently rolling vineyards provide excellent drainage and give the vines access to the underlying limestone.
Photographs by Steven Elphick

and syrah benefitting from cooling, water-cresting breezes. The newest vineyard, Limestone Ridge, is located on a beautifully sloping ridge above the village of Jordon. Each sub-appellation offers unique characteristics, creating matchless flavors and nuances within bottles of repeating varietals.

Constructed with locally quarried limestone and native wood, the winery is a classic representation of natural resources and beauty. Multiple levels encased in glass supply soothing vantage points of a serene pond beyond. Visitors can also see vines happily growing in their intended habitat while sheep graze peacefully on unwanted foliage beneath them. A horse and plough—a delightful alternative to common machinery—are often spotted preparing the land for new plantings. The property is also home to tall, broad, and strong shire-bred livestock that are considered family and treated accordingly. Fortunate visitors are able to meet them up close—a rare treat—and admire their stunning and graceful demeanor. Celebrated as an estate holiday, an annual concert series is held during the summer solstice and is ideal for a weekend of local culinary treats and live music in the vineyards.

Top: The wine library contains examples of virtually all the wines ever made at Tawse.

Middle: The retail store has a comprehensive view of both the production operations and the grounds.

Bottom: The six-level, gravity-fed production facility allows Mother Nature to do most of the work.

Facing Page: Justin and Casey, the winery's horses, help with tending the vineyard.

Previous Pages: The cellar tasting room includes the extensive wine library, where back vintages are stored.
Photographs by Steven Elphick

Cherry Avenue Pinot Noir
Pair with seasoned filet of beef or pork, roasted chicken with herbs, or duck confit.

Tawse Riesling
Pair with a fresh salad with vinaigrette dressing, raw oysters, cream cheeses, and assortments of seafood.

Tawse Meritage
Pair with jalapeño-wrapped steak strips and fire-roasted potatoes.

Tastings
Open to the public daily, year-round

CHERRY AVE **T** VINEYARD

ESTATE BOTTLED

TAWSE 2009

PINOT NOIR

VQA TWENTY MILE BENCH VQA

PROPRIETOR

750mL   RED WINE / VIN ROUGE / PRODUCT OF CANADA / PRODUIT DU CANADA   13% alc./vol.

Vineland Estates Winery

Vineland

Vineland Estates Winery is truly one of Canada's best destination wineries, with a rich history dating back to 1845. Owned by the DeGasperis family from Toronto and managing partner and president Allan Schmidt, the vineyard and winery were originally established by Herman Weis, with plantings of the Weis 21 clone of riesling spread across 75 acres. Hailing from the Mosel region in Germany, Herman was an experienced grower with a keen sense of Niagara's terroir and what varietals would thrive there. His early 1978 plantings continue to grow some of Canada's most notable riesling today, processed by current winemaker Brian Schmidt. Brian is developing distinctive riesling, chardonnay, and cabernet franc, and recently brought home Canada's first Premio Speciale Gran VinItaly award as the highest-scoring winery in the world.

Brothers Allan and Brian Schmidt have been actively responsible for the success of the vineyard and winery since 1987. Third-generation grape growers and winemakers, Allan and Brian were born and raised in the Okanagan Valley of British Columbia. After completing enological training in California at Heitz Cellars and viticulture training in the Nahe region of Germany, Allan moved to Ontario to become the winemaker and general manager of Vineland Estates Winery. Meanwhile, Brian traveled extensively throughout Europe to study winemaking and joined his brother in Ontario in 1991. He became the winemaker just three years later while Allan became president.

Top: Uncork Vineland Estates wines and experience some of the best of what Niagara wine country has to offer.

Bottom: The winery produces an array of award-winning VQA wines.

Facing Page: Vineland Estates wine barrels are stored in underground cellars for the best results.
Photographs by Steven Elphick

Offering minerality and balanced acidity, the estate's wines are counted among Niagara's best. Producing 50,000 cases of wine annually, the vineyard is located within the Niagara Escarpment sub-appellation Twenty Mile Bench. Vines are overseen by consultant Roman Prydatkewycz, who has many years of experience growing his own grapes in Niagara. While the riesling is consistently rated among the best in Ontario, premium bottles of chardonnay, sauvignon blanc, cabernet franc, and red Bordeaux blends also receive greatly deserved praise, including over a hundred international awards. The winery's most popular exports include its famous icewines and VICE—a 21-percent alcohol Canadian vodka and vidal icewine blend.

The estate extends far beyond a winery, with gourmet dining, overnight accommodations, a wine store with cheese market, and event facilities. Housed in renovated structures original to the property, tastings, shopping, dining, weddings, and corporate functions take on new charm. A stone building circa 1850, the Carriage House is an intimate space providing dazzling views of flourishing vines and foliage, wonderful for weddings and receptions. Post-nuptials, brides and grooms are welcome to spend the night in a private bed-and-breakfast cottage, just steps away. The one-bedroom chalet contains a kitchen and a lounge area where couples can get comfortable with a complimentary bottle of wine. Family and friends can take advantage of an estate guest house with three bedrooms, a large lounge area, and a kitchen, safely distanced from the newlyweds.

Right: The wine shop is housed in a beautiful log barn built in 1857.

Facing Page Top: Vineland Estates Winery occupies historic estate farm buildings dating back to 1857.

Facing Page Bottom: The Carriage House is perfect for private functions.
Photographs by Steven Elphick

Four-diamond dining and an onsite market with wine shop satisfy epicurean curiosities and gourmet cravings. Dinner inside of an 1845 farmhouse, or beneath an umbrella of trees, is served by an internationally trained team of chefs—led by executive chef Justin Downes—that perfectly pairs innovative creations with estate mainstays like VICE, the world's first vodka and icewine concoction. The winery retail shop and market occupy a century-old barn built in 1877 that was once used to store farm equipment. Fully restored to its former glory, the wine shop and tasting bar are located on the lower floor while the market is just above, carrying a vast selection of local artisan cheeses, gourmet foods, and kitchen essentials for perusing, discovering, and most importantly, tasting.

Above Left: Niagara regional cuisine is created by chef Justin Downes.

Above Right: Guests are invited to dine onsite at one of the top 20 winery restaurants in the world.

Left: Allan Schmidt is Vineland Estates Winery's president.

Facing Page: The famous St. Urban Estate Vineyard was planted in 1978.
Photographs by Steven Elphick

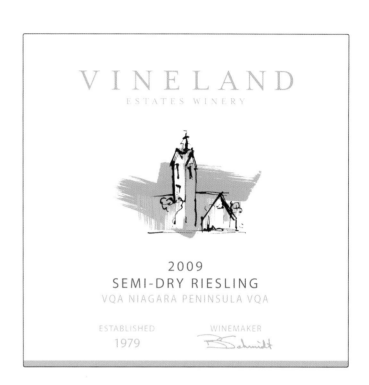

Semi-Dry Riesling
Pair with grilled fish and lemon.

Cabernet Franc
Pair with tomato-based pasta or grilled pork.

VICE
Pair with fresh oysters.

Tastings
Open to the public daily, seasonally

Rosehall Run Vineyards, page 238

Lacey Estates Winery, page 234

The Grange of Prince Edward Vineyards and Estate Winery, page 246

Hillier Creek Estates

Hillier

The underground water sources in Prince Edward County percolate through a maze of fractured limestone on their journey toward Lake Ontario. In a couple of rare spots in the region, the water finds its way to the surface, emerging in the form of streams such as Hillier Creek. The abundant natural water source on the property makes it ideal for supporting grapes; that's been the case since as far back as the late 1800s, when the original landowner, Dorland Noxon, won a winemaking medal at the 1876 Philadelphia International Exhibition. In recent years, the region around Hillier has become synonymous with excellent pinot noirs and elegant chardonnays. Given the area's geological, topographical, and climactic similarities to the Burgundy region of France, wines from Hillier are able to stand shoulder to shoulder with some of the finer wines in the world.

In his youth, Hillier Creek Estates' owner Kemp Stewart spent six years traveling around Europe, receiving an informal education in the finest wines the continent had to offer. Later he and his wife Amber became avid collectors, learning about grape varieties, styles, techniques, and auspicious winemaking regions. In 1999, while living in Kingston, the couple caught wind of some buzz about a winery opening in nearby Prince Edward County. The news revived Kemp's long-held winemaking fantasies and, after spending the summer of 2000 searching, the duo purchased the 50-acre property with rolling hills more reminiscent of a classic European vineyard than the typically flat Prince Edward County.

Top and Bottom: Owner Kemp Stewart is proud of his 100-percent estate-grown grapes.

Facing page: The view from the patio is beautiful.
Photographs by Steven Elphick

Unfortunately, the buildings had not been inhabited for 15 years; bringing them up to speed while still retaining the personality of the land would become a decade-long challenge. The Stewarts spent the next six years installing weeping-tile, clearing plate limestone from the soil, planting vines across 27 acres, and restoring the property's 160-year-old barn. In 2006, the duo brought on vineyard manager Woody Cassell and sold their first small harvest to local wineries. Two years later the barn restoration was complete, and in 2010 the Stewarts brought in winemaker Ben Simmons and opened the estate's doors to the public with a selection of pinot noir, gamay, chardonnay, vidal, and a riesling that has sold out every year since.

Today that restored dairy barn serves as Hillier Creek Estates' sophisticated winery and tasting room. Above the bar, a 12-foot oil painting of a herd of cows hints at the structure's humble roots. Inside, guests taste and compare notes as sunlight streams through the tasting room's rustic structure. The presence of natural light serves as a constant reminder of one of the area's most important natural advantages: abundant levels of sunlight. And, as any vintner will tell you, the more sunlight, the higher the sugar levels and the better the wine.

Top: A restored dairy barn is the perfect place to host an event at Hillier Creek Estates.

Bottom and Facing Page Top: Hillier Creek Estates' chardonnay and gamay are favorites to sample in the tasting room.

Facing Page Bottom: The rolling vines can be seen from the patio.
Photographs by Steven Elphick

Hillier Creek Estates is one of the growing number of wineries taking full advantage of the industry's technological advances. The estate's harvester can turn over 32 tons of grapes in 11 hours, nearly eliminating the potential for an unexpected weather hazard endangering the entire crop, and the mobile bottling system enables Kemp and his team to fill, cork, label, and package the entire year's production in about two days. Hillier Creek Estate's wines have been strong right out of the gate. The estate's 2007 vidal icewine was awarded the gold from the 2010 Finger Lakes International Wine Competition; the 2007 pinot noir and 2008 chardonnay brought home the bronze.

Winemaking in Prince Edward County is not for the faint of heart; as an estate, 100 percent of Hillier Creek Estates grapes must be grown—and the wines must be made—on the property, a challenging task in an area that has a reputation for temperamental weather patterns. But the terroir produces a product that is known for good structure and lots of personality—a winning combination that makes that decade of preparation worthwhile.

Above: Guests can enjoy 100-percent estate-grown wine on the county's prettiest patio.

Facing Page: Visitors are encouraged to explore, experience, and enjoy at Hillier Creek Estates. *Photographs by Steven Elphick*

Barrel-Aged Chardonnay

The creamy yet elegant structure, with aromas of vanilla and cooked pear, is delightful with a mushroom alfredo pasta or as an aperitif with a triple crème Brie.

Rosé

The strawberry aroma and pink grapefruit flavor provide the perfect counterbalance to a spicy stir-fry.

Gamay

A peppery nose and cranberry and cherry aromas make this wine ideal alongside a bruschetta appetizer or Thanksgiving turkey.

Tastings

Open to the public daily May through October and on weekends November through December, March through April

Huff Estates Winery
Bloomfield

Everyone dreams of having their little own corner of the world. Lanny Huff, owner and sole proprietor of Huff Estates Winery, actually has one. Established in 2004, the winery sits on a little bit of Ontario called Huff Corners; it once belonged to members of Lanny's family. Before he purchased the land back, it had changed hands several times, having been used previously as fields for cash crops. When the area was determined to be a prime location for vineyards, Lanny did not hesitate to take advantage of the opportunity. Huff Estates sits in the heart of Prince Edward County, where Lanny was born and raised. After traveling the world and developing a passion and palate for fine wines, it only made sense for Lanny to search his homeland for the perfect soil match for vines.

The winery's facility is housed in a modern building that utilizes natural gravity flow in temperature-controlled barrel cellars to store the wine. Winemaker Frédéric "Fred" Picard has been with Huff Estates since its establishment. Fred studied at the Lycée of Beaune, where he completed his winemaking enology degree. As a winemaker, he has created vintages in France, Italy, South Africa, Chile, California, and Niagara. In addition to Fred's expertise, general manager Jason Sharpe holds a Masters of Wine Business from the University of Adelaide in Australia. Vineyard manager Alex Hunter is a member of the first graduating class of the Niagara College Winery and Viticulture Technician program. The experts at Huff Estates work together to produce an array of varietals: chardonnay, pinot gris, pinot noir, cabernet franc, merlot, vidal, and frontenac gris. The winery specializes in chardonnay, sparkling wine, and pinot gris and has produced a number of national award-winning vintages, such as the Cuvée Peter F. Huff, which has won gold and double gold medals for various vintages as well as the Lieutenant Governor's Award for Excellence in Ontario Wines.

Top: In the corridor at the Inn at Huff Estates is a wall-mounted limestone waterfall set behind a steel "H."

Bottom: Huff Estates is built into the side of a hill, thus the gravity-fed barrel cellar is located just behind the tasting room and is six feet underground.

Facing Page: The contemporary entrance at Huff Estates' retail store glows at night.
Photographs by Steven Elphick

Huff Estates is home to two vineyards in the Prince Edward County appellation. The South Bay Vineyard spans 25 acres and is located in the southeastern corner of the county, surrounded by Lake Ontario and South Bay. Ancient oak trees provide a natural windbreak, which protects the grapes. The temperate climate provided by the nearby water likewise provides an ideal location for the growth and maturation of several varietals, including cabernet franc, merlot, pinot noir, chardonnay, and pinot gris.

The 62 & 1 Vineyard, named after its crossroads location, surrounds the winery, the Inn at Huff Estates, and the Oeno Gallery. The terroir of this vineyard lends a unique acidity and minerality to the wines produced from the pinot gris, pinot noir, vidal, and frontenac gris grown at the site. The vineyard's north-south alignment and slope provide optimal sun exposure for ripening.

Top: Owner and president Lanny Huff was born and raised in Prince Edward County.

Bottom: The national award-winning Cuvée Peter F. Huff and South Bay Chardonnay are flagship wines.

Facing Page: The suspended ceiling and zinc tasting bar make for a unique tasting experience.
Photographs by Steven Elphick

If visitors to the winery wish to find accommodations, Huff Estates provides that as well. The Inn at Huff Estates features a limited number of contemporary country suites. Also nestled in the 62 & 1 Vineyard is the Oeno Gallery, which displays contemporary art primarily from Canadian artists.

The winery hosts various wine-centric events throughout the year, but the facility is most proud of 6 Barrels for 6 Chefs. The event was started in 2006 by Huff Estates winemaker Fred and renowned Canadian chef Bryan Steele. The annual festivities feature six wine and food stations manned by six different chefs who have created recipes that pair specifically with their assigned wine. It provides guests with a unique opportunity to experience various interpretations of the Huff Estates wines.

Top: The Inn at Huff Estates is nestled amongst the vines and offers unique, contemporary accommodations.

Middle: The 1,100-square-foot bedroom of the winemaker's suite is a favorite at the Inn at Huff Estates.

Bottom: An asparagus and goat cheese creation by chef Michael Hoy of Hoy at Huff.

Facing Page: The four-acre sculpture garden at Huff Estates has a quarter mile of pathway, 35,000 flowers, and 40 sculptures by local, national, and international artists.
Photographs by Steven Elphick

South Bay Chardonnay
Pair with asparagus and lobster crêpes with
fines herbs Hollandaise sauce.

Cuvee Peter Huff
Delicious with honeyed figs with prosciutto and basil.

Pinot Gris
Pair with grilled halibut with lemon, dill, and cucumber sauce.

Merlot Reserve
Perfect with braised veal with portobello mushrooms,
celery root, and toasted pecans.

Tastings
Open to the public daily

Karlo Estates

Prince Edward County

At Karlo Estates, it's possible to taste delicious Prince Edward County wine, view works of art in a restored barn, hike, picnic, and simply relax while enjoying nature—all in one place. Master winemaker, wine judge, and owner Richard Karlo had been making wine to great acclaim for 20 years prior to purchasing the 93-acre property in 2005. Open to the public since 2010, the winery produces the largest portfolio of unique premium wines in Prince Edward County.

The Karlo Estates land was first deeded in 1799 to Peter VanAlstine, the leader of the original Loyalist group that landed in the area in 1784. Widely known throughout Prince Edward County as one of the key figures in the early days, he built the Glenora Mill, launched the Glenora Ferry, and was appointed the first member of Parliament for the region; the land was his reward. After his death in 1800, the Stevenson family purchased the land and owned it until 2005, when Richard and partner Sherry Martin acquired it. The two, fond of the rural region and lifestyle, were drawn to the property's beauty and grape growing potential. To that end they built drystone walls as an entrance between the historic barn and the road. In 2007, in conjunction with the Drystone Wall Association of Canada, they built the largest drystone bridge in North America over Hubbs Creek running beside the vineyard. Drystone, an ancient method of building widely used in Richard's maternal family home in England's Lake District, involves constructing structures with no mortar, fitting the stones together like a puzzle. Richard's background in civil engineering led him to renovate the barn as a winery. The circa-1845 barn houses wine production tanks and barrels in the original milking salon, tastings in the main area, and an art studio with works by artist Sherry Martin in the Loft Gallery above.

Top: Founder and winemaker Richard Karlo.

Bottom: Partner and artist Sherry Martin in the Loft Gallery studio working on a portrait of Veronica Andersson.

Facing Page: The renovated barn winery and drystone wall at Karlo Estates.
Photographs by Steven Elphick

Off the back of the barn guests discover a greenhouse-style post-and-beam sun deck, perfect for wine tasting year-round. All wine tastings are paired with food to enhance the experience.

Located slightly north of Lake Ontario, the south-sloping, gently rolling terrain is composed of Hillier clay loam limestone soil. An ancient seabed contributed the limestone, which infuses minerality into the Burgundian-like soil. There are currently two vineyard blocks totaling 11 acres planted, with more going in each year. In 2006, the first three-and-a-half acres of pinot noir, chardonnay, and frontenac noir were planted, with more pinot noir plus frontenac gris, frontenac blanc, and marquette added

later. Wine production began in 2008; Richard crafts his vintages with an eye to Old World, artisanal practices. However, he's a true pioneer who took frontenac noir and marquette grapes and created the region's first port—named, appropriately, after Peter VanAlstine and chosen as one of the top 10 cutting-edge wines in the world at 2010's Gourmet Food & Wine Expo in Toronto. Richard also fermented chardonnay in CHOA barrels—cherry, hickory, oak, and ash—to create a unique style. Other offerings include Bordeaux varietals like cabernet sauvignon, cabernet franc, malbec, and

Above: The 1845 barn, with its sundeck, is a beautiful sight for guests.

Right: Visitors are invited to sit and stay awhile to enjoy tastings with food pairings on the sundeck.

Facing Page: The main tasting bar with Sherry's Loft Gallery studio above.
Photographs by Steven Elphick

merlot, barrel-fermented riesling, pinot noir, a frontenac gris rosé, five-varietal blend Quintus, and a petit verdot single-varietal wine called The 5th Element. One of the very first Ontario white port-style wines rounds out the unique selections.

The wines, produced in limited quantities, are lower in alcohol with a restrained use of oak. The mineral-rich soil and cool climate give the wines higher acidity and more complexity for great food pairings. All grapes are hand-picked, many wild fermented, and unfiltered; long cool ferments produce fuller-bodied wines.

Sherry designs the wine labels, which feature drawings of the drystone bridge or Celtic symbols in honor of the partners' shared Celtic heritage. With so many different wines to try, the diverse portfolio attracts many visitors, and the expansive property truly has something for everyone.

Top: In the tasting room's music corner, anyone who plays a song is rewarded with a free tasting.
Photograph by Steven Elphick

Middle: "Little Bug" greets customers when she isn't keeping an eye on the wine.
Photograph by Kari MacKnight

Bottom: Karlo Estates' very popular VanAlstine Port.
Photograph by Steven Elphick

Facing Page: North America's largest drystone bridge spans Hubbs Creek at the end of the vineyard.
Photograph by Steven Elphick

The 5th Element
(100% petit verdot)
A great steak wine with a peppery nose and clean acidity; also has exotic notes of cardamom, cassis, and chocolate that pair well with Indian curries.

Lake on the Mountain Riesling
Slightly off-dry with bright acidity pairing well with fettuccine alfredo or spicy foods like Thai or Asian cuisine.

VanAlstine Port
Classically pairs with Stilton cheese, walnuts, fresh figs, and a fine cigar; Also great with chocolate molten lava cake, raspberry sorbet or fresh berries with Mascarpone.

Tastings
Open to the public daily, seasonally

Lacey Estates Winery

Hillier

Charles Lacey, CEO of Lacey Estates Winery, is the product of a hard-working mother and a character-building life. Born in Wales and raised in Morocco, he landed in Canada mid-century and worked as an electrician for more than 50 years. It was during these labor-intensive times that Charles discovered Prince Edward County and its pristine terrain. During a work-related assignment he came upon an 18th-century farm beckoning for attention. Seduced by the promise of a blissful retirement, Charles and his wife Mollie purchased the farm as a rustic withdraw from the bustle of city life and two years later purchased the 58 acres adjacent to the farm, as they did not want structures neighboring their historic retreat.

It wasn't until a local wine seminar exposed Charles and his son Kimball to the clay loam over limestone earth found in Hillier that a family vineyard seemed advantageous. The farm became an estate with eight acres of vines. Fostered by Charles and Mollie, along with their family, Kimball, Andrew, and Liz, the vines became a labor of love and, consequently, parting with the resulting grapes was unthinkable. In 2009, a winery constructed of refurbished materials original to the 18th-century farm, like century-old maple flooring preserved from the dining room and ancient granite hand-shaped by a local stone mason, was opened to the public. Complete with a renovated tasting bar and turn-of-the-century décor, the interior is a soulful collection of preserved pieces, perfect for enjoying one of Kimball's tasty creations.

Top and Bottom: Pinot noir grapes bloom on the vine while waiting for harvest. Once plucked, the supple juice is pressed from their skins during crush.

Facing Page: After aging in oak barrels and steel tanks, the wine is bottled, labeled, and corked for future enjoyment.
Photographs by Steven Elphick

Kimball earned a grape and wine certificate from the University of Guelph and continued his education working with Norm Hardie for four years and then as associate winemaker with Closson Chase. He continues to work there today, sharing his talents and time with two estates.

Marking 100-percent estate-made bottles of riesling, gewürztraminer, baco noir, chardonnay, pinot gris, and pinot noir, a redesigned family crest acts as the estate label and is reminiscent of the authentic one. The "L"—painted as a grapevine—rests above former cannonballs-turned-grapes, depicted in purple as a sign of British royalty. As the label indicates, each bottle possesses certain nobility from the quality of the grape, the distinction of the terroir, and the promise of the hands behind it all.

Top: Steel tanks and oak barrels nurture the wines into maturation.

Middle: Kimball Lacey, winemaker at the estate, received an Intervin International bronze medal for his 2009 baco noir.

Bottom: The simple tasting room at Lacey Estates is free of ornamentation, allowing the raw but polished materials to reflect the natural terrain outdoors while presenting estate tastings.

Facing Page: The freshly picked gewürztraminer grape originated in Austria and produces a very aromatic, full-bodied white wine.
Photographs by Steven Elphick

Pinot Gris
Pair with chicken Marsala over fettuccine or linguini.

Riesling
Pair with seared scallops and apple slaw.

Pinot Noir
Pair with rosemary and garlic roasted lamb with potatoes au gratin.

Baco Noir
Pair with Kobe beef and wild mushroom stew.

Tastings
Open to the public daily, year-round

Rosehall Run Vineyards

Wellington

Situated near the small hamlet of Rosehall, just west of Wellington in Prince Edward County, the scenic property of Rosehall Run Vineyards began as a working farm, producing crops such as tomatoes, corn, hay, and soy. An old tractor and farmhouse, relics of the site's former life, stand in testament to years of toiling in the adaptable soil. In 2000, Dan and Lynn Sullivan, with their partner Cam Reston, purchased the 150-acre farm for the purpose of growing grapes, and a winery ensued.

What began as a modest barn processing center—including wine production and barrel storage—became a 7,200-square-foot elaborate facility complete with a barrel cellar blasted deep into the limestone foundation. A modern tasting room constructed of eco-friendly materials such as cork, Kirei board, and straw fabric soon followed. Its warm appeal is furthered by the details, such as a locally constructed, three-tiered chandelier made of dried grape vines original to the property. Its intricate formation is disarming and interesting, just as the artist intended. Sizeable glass doors allow an abundance of light and views of the vineyards to come through.

Remarkable estate vintages, such as chardonnay and pinot noir, have received a plurality of awards along with notable commendations from aficionados in Canada, California, New York, and England.

Top: Grapes are gently harvested by hand and processed with care, ensuring healthy fruit bearing robust flavors.

Bottom: Owner and winemaker Dan Sullivan takes a hands-on approach when it comes to the vineyard. Daily walks and inspections keep him in-tune with the needs and wants of his favored fruit.

Facing Page: Nestled among Prince Edward County's rolling terrain, the vineyards are planted on 150 acres of unspoiled farmland.
Photographs by Steven Elphick

Proactive in the community, Rosehall Run participates in Prince Edward County community projects each year. As proud sponsors of the Festival Players of Prince Edward County, the winery offers an intimate setting for guests to enjoy local talent and wine. Additionally, Dan works as a passionate ambassador for the Ontario wine industry. Along with local and international chefs, restaurateurs, and fellow winemakers, Rosehall Run is committed to elevating Ontario's thriving local food and wine scene to national recognition and beyond.

At times, the 10-year journey from purchasing unplanted farmland to producing internationally recognized wine was both surprisingly fast and painfully slow for Lynn and Dan—who had never before even operated a tractor. With a "two steps forward and one step back" approach, they forged the path together, navigating local marketing channels and relying on the support and expertise of fellow partner Cam Reston.

Above: Owner and winemaker Dan Sullivan welcomes guests to his idea of paradise: a glass of Cuvée County 100-percent Prince Edward County pinot noir, pinot gris, or chardonnay.

Left and Facing Page: The winery's tasting room is visually and tangibly stunning, boasting honey-colored wood, soft lighting, and an abundance of glass. Exposed rows of wine showcase the estate's vintages within a clever, cellar-like design.
Photographs by Steven Elphick

Pinot Noir
Pair with seared duck breast with Montmorency sauce and celeriac purée.

Chardonnay
Pair with lobster ravioli in fennel and chervil-infused cream sauce.

Sullyzwicker Red
Pair with beans slow-cooked with garlic, herb sprigs, bay leaves, celery, potatoes, and tomatoes. Serve with toasted sourdough bread.

Tastings
Open daily, year-round

ROSEHALL RUN
VINEYARDS INC.

Sandbanks Estate Winery

Wellington

Named after beautiful Sandbanks Provincial Park, Sandbanks Estate Winery is a popular stop for tourists who are drawn to the seductive year-round scenery. With miles of sandy beaches and sparkling water, the park is a showpiece of the celebrated Prince Edward County, known equally for its picturesque countryside, lush farmland, and charming villages. Winemaker Catherine Langlois was enchanted by the unparalleled surroundings from her first visit to what is known by many as simply "The County." Her joyful energy, infatuation with the terrain, and the area's active lifestyle served as inspiration for the initial planting of six acres of varietals in 2000.

Respected within the Canadian wine scene for well over a decade and a skilled winemaker trained in the fields of Quebec and Burgundy, Catherine followed her passion to pursue the apex of her craft: a winery of her own in the setting of her dreams. The Sandbanks vineyard is located just outside of Wellington, facing the lake where the water reflects the changing hues of an endless sky. Planted with hybrids and vinifera, the vineyard produces varietals such as riesling, chardonnay, vidal, Geisenheim, pinot noir, cabernet franc, baco noir, and maréchal foch, which mature in Hillier clay loam infused with high lime content ideal for growing and producing quality wines. Moderating influences, courtesy of the Great Lake, help protect the fruit from spring frost, and with the vineyard's south-facing slope overlooking the water, the vineyard also benefits from ideal drainage.

Top: Sandbanks Estate Winery offers a lovely series of white wines, including Waves, Dunes, and Shoreline White.

Bottom: A juicy bunch of Geisenheim grapes are ripe for plucking.

Facing Page: A colorful collection of Adirondack chairs face the shoreline and welcome guests outside for views of the water.
Photographs by Steven Elphick

Specifically chosen for its ability to ripen early, the baco noir grapes promise desired sugar levels and produce a reliable crop every year, even in frosty Canadian winters. Considered to be the winery's signature variety, baco noir is a full-bodied wine with intense plum and wild cherry flavors that receives abundant and well-deserved praise. In fact, it won the gold medal People's Choice Award at TASTE!, a premier culinary event celebrating regional food and drink.

Other varieties at Sandbanks, such as maréchal foch and cabernet franc, garner equal support from a loyal cult following. The winery has even received noble admiration from Queen Elizabeth II, who sampled Shoreline Red—a cabernet merlot cuvée—as well as a bottle of Dunes—a vidal with a splash of riesling—during a recent visit to Ottawa. Both received royal approval.

A depth of community as generous as the breadth of wine offerings exists at Sandbanks Winery. It hosts a permanent art exhibit and numerous public events, including harvest parties, Spanish fiestas, campfire and open mic nights, wine release parties, and art shows for avid attendees and newcomers alike.

Whether in the fields of vines heavy with fruit or inside the winery, where walls are adorned with the vibrant paintings of artist-in-residence Rita Thivierge, Sandbanks Winery exudes the joyful life, warmth, and distinction that has become synonymous with its outstanding wines.

Top: A new-age boutique, adorned with artist Rita Thivierge's vibrant paintings, contains a bright and engaging interior.

Middle: Rita Thivierge's abstract landscapes burst with color and bring the winery walls to life.

Bottom: The sun-filled patio faces west, into endless acres of verdant and thriving vines.

Facing Page: The rocky shoreline offers front-row seating for daily sunsets into Lake Ontario's calm waters.
Photographs by Steven Elphick

Dunes
Pair with a sampling of cheeses or grilled fish or poultry.

Cabernet Franc
Pair with rich goat cheese and aged Cheddar.

Baco Noir
Pair with beef-layered lasagna or spaghetti with meat sauce.

Mouton Noir
Pair with braised lamb, mushroom ravioli, and decadent dark chocolate.

Tastings
Open to the public daily, seasonally

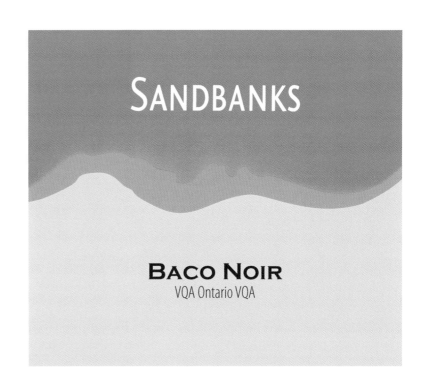

The Grange of Prince Edward Vineyards and Estate Winery

Hillier

For Robert Granger, farming was not only a choice, it was his destiny. In addition to being born with the Granger namesake—which means farmer—Robert hails from a lineage of agricultural-loving ancestors, which probably explains how his family received its name. Robert warmly recalls a childhood spent with his grandfather toiling away on the land. A great distance from his position as a corporate and securities lawyer, returning to working the earth was always his dream, in addition to one day reconnecting with his home-grown heritage. As serendipity would have it, a summer afternoon drive in 1970 delivered Robert to his destiny when he and his wife Diana happened upon the Trumpour farm in Ontario. They were immediately enamored by its natural splendor and purchased the property as a family retreat.

Renamed The Grange in homage to the Granger family heritage and also to the generations of farmers that labored land before them, the property became a weekend escape for the family to work, recharge, and devour Prince Edward County's rich history. It wasn't until daughter Caroline Grace Granger moved her family to the site in 1997 that the idea for a farm-to-vineyard conversion was first flirted with. For two centuries, the area had served an assortment of purposes, from a saw mill and a dairy farm to a chicken canning operation. Its versatile past and proven success—even during the Great Depression—gave Caroline confidence that a transformation from utilitarian farm to relevant vineyard was a delicious decision.

Top: The Trumpour's Mill series at The Grange offers seven varietals—including the consistently dynamic pinot noir—many of which are available throughout Ontario and LCBO outlets.

Bottom: Growing prolifically in Northfield's fourth vineyard block, cabernet franc grapes are ready for harvest.

Facing Page: The Grange, in all its glory, overlooks a peaceful pond where turtles sun and geese sometimes settle to raise their young.
Photographs by Steven Elphick

The first vineyard was planted with 12 acres of chardonnay, gamay, and pinot noir grapes in 2001. Over the years, the one vineyard expanded into six with a respectable 60 acres of varietals including pinot gris, riesling, cabernet franc, and sauvignon blanc. Guests are invited to try the estate's 100-percent VQA-certified sustainable and estate-grown wines inside the property's renovated barn. Dating back to 1826, it has previously been used for milking cows and storing hay, and is now a genteel winery presenting prominent wines—like *Food & Drink* magazine's favorite, pinot gris—to curious consumers.

These days Caroline has her hands full as president and CEO of a successful agribusiness. Whether she is working at the winery with her daughter Maggie— the eldest of three—or serving on one of the many councils, committees, and associations that she is a member of, it is all for the benefit of Ontario's prolific wine industry and Canada's agricultural development.

Top: A shaded patio with views of the pond invites guests to linger with a glass of wine or a casual country lunch.

Middle Left: Shelves of wines hold a complete collection of Trumpour's Mill bottles and display a number of award-winning vintages in the hayloft-turned-tasting room.

Middle Right: Delicate pinot noir clusters hang in wait for harvest within the winery's oldest vineyard, Diana block.

Bottom: Once filled with bales of hay from floor to beam, the winery now welcomes visitors eager to taste wine and escape the daily grind.

Facing Page: Looking down Northfield into the Victoria block, rows of vines stretch across two kilometers of planted land.
Photographs by Steven Elphick

Gamay
Sip with roasted wild turkey and scalloped potatoes garnished with gamay jelly.

Pinot Gris
Pair with spicy chicken pad Thai and steamed edamame.

Brut
Drink with oysters on the half shell and boiled jumbo shrimp.

Pinot Noir
Sip with lamb kabobs grilled with red peppers and onions over risotto.

Tastings
Open to the public daily, year-round

Viewpointe Estate Winery, page 270

Pelee Island Winery, page 264

Cooper's Hawk Vineyards, page 258

Colio Estate Wines

Harrow

Since its inception in 1980, Colio Estate Wines has captured hundreds of awards the world over and was named Winery of the Year by the Niagara Grape and Wine Festival. Co-owned by José Berardo and his business partner Enzo DeLuca—son of the original founder Alfredo DeLuca—the winery and its name pay homage to the great Collio Gorizian, an Italian wine-producing region within Friuli-Venezia Giulia. Its multi-peaked façade, with Douglas fir timber and flagstone design, reflects the founders' roots in northern Italy and Canada, where they built their winery.

Prior to Prohibition, the region now known as the Lake Erie North Shore was the largest commercial grape growing area in the country. The land is well suited for viticulture since it is located on the same latitude as Northern California and Tuscany. In 1980, Colio received the first winery license in the region since Prohibition. Today the Colio estate vineyards in Colchester sit at 41.59 degrees north latitude and benefit from southern exposure from Lake Erie, which allows for one of the longest growing seasons in the country. This region is ideal for growing the Bordeaux varietals such as cabernet franc, merlot, and cabernet sauvignon, but it is also favorable for shiraz, sauvignon blanc, chardonnay, riesling, and pinot grigio. Colio Estate Wines' 200 acres of vineyards are expertly managed by Kevin Donohue.

Top: The winery's hospitality center is finished in custom stained-glass windows that feature unique Douglas fir gables.

Bottom: The building façade employs stone and wood elements to symbolize the founders' roots in Italy and the Canadian countryside where the winery is located.

Facing Page: Colio Estate Wines opened its doors in in 1980.
Photographs by Steven Elphick

All great wineries begin with a great winemaker. Lured away from one of the most reputable wineries in Italy, Colio's original master winemaker, Carlo Negri, applied a blend of time-honored traditional methods with technological innovation until his retirement in 2009. His work earned him and the winery hundreds of awards, including the Ontario Wine Awards Winemaker of the Year and the Tony Aspler Cuvée Award of Excellence.

Today Lawrence Buhler leads the winery as vice president of winemaking and presides over several brand families that encompass VQA table wine, sparkling wine, and icewine. The winery's portfolio includes its ultra-premium Colio Estate Vineyards (CEV) series, the wildly popular Girls' Night Out VQA and flavored wines, and the Lake and River series of VQA table wines, among others.

While CEV is the estate's signature line of limited edition and ultra-premium offerings, the Girls' Night Out series has garnered great attention as one of the first VQA concept wines. Colio Lake and River is the winery's value-priced VQA wine family, and the company also produces a popular line of sparkling, fresh-fruit-flavored non-alcoholic wines called St. Tropez.

Above: Nestled by the Lake Erie shoreline in the hamlet of Colchester, Colio's 200 acres of estate vineyards bask under the most sun hours in the country.
Photograph by Steven Elphick

Right: As vice president, Lawrence Buhler brings an innate passion to the company's winemaking and presides over its 330,000 cases of wine produced annually.
Photograph by Courtney Sendzik

Facing Page: Aside from the winery's estate CEV wines, the company produces several other labels of award-winning wines, including the Girls' Night Out series.
Photograph by Steven Elphick

The charming winery in Harrow has a total cooperage of 2.4 million liters of wine in stainless steel tanks or European and American oak barrels, which age gracefully in a climate-controlled cellar. A modern bottling line that produces upward of 330,000 cases per year completes the state-of-the-art setup.

Visitors can enjoy tastings and tours at the stylish hospitality center, which features a complete collection of estate wines, wine-related gifts, and souvenirs. Here quality wines of sound value engage both neophytes and well-versed collectors. Plans to expand the winery's interests include constructing a showcase winery and distillery on a parcel of land in Niagara-on-the-Lake, thereby securing a significant presence in two of the most important VQA regions in the country and making the company's wines more accessible to its ever-increasing following.

Top: Warm, friendly, and inviting, the hospitality center is a welcoming start and finish to the Colio experience.

Middle: The humidity controlled barrel cellar is ideal for the aging of wines that will eventually find their way into the company's award-winning premium products.

Bottom: Hand-carved wooden mammoths keep vigil over the barrel cellar.

Facing Page: The sun sinks into the western sky, having spent the day in its usual ripening mode.
Photographs by Steven Elphick

CEV Reserve Cabernet Franc
Pair with roasted venison in a demi-glaze with black currants.

Lake and River Moonlight White
Pair with sushi or fresh fish.

Girls' Night Out Sparkling
Pair with smoked salmon, capers, cream cheese, lemon,
and pepper on toasted baguette.

CEV Vidal Icewine
Pair with Gorgonzola cheese and peach coulis.

Tastings
Open to the public daily, year-round

Cooper's Hawk Vineyards

Harrow

Years of jet-setting and accommodating a fast-paced career led Tom O'Brien to a rural retirement. While traveling the world over offered many advantages—such as experiencing other cultures—it lost its luster after almost a decade of in-flight living. One of the many benefits of these years on the road was an exposure to and resulting affinity for wine. No stranger to Napa, Sonoma, France, or Italy, Tom became interested in cultivating a sustainable property to retire on, with the possibility of grapes.

Taken by the lush landscape and signs of life on 68 sprawling acres of Lake Erie's North Shore, Tom found his version of paradise. Acquired from a farmer, some of the property had been used as an apple orchard, while most of it was virgin terrain. With the hope of appealing to local wineries, Tom appointed 10 acres of the land to be a vineyard and invested two long years into its transformation. With the support of his wife Katy, son Mike, and daughters Erin and Meagan, Tom redirected his original plans to sell the grapes and established a winery instead.

Cooper's Hawk Vineyards is a leading source for estate-grown cabernet, merlot, chardonnay, riesling, and cabernet franc grapes. The rapidly expanding vineyard has chardonnay musqué and pinot noir lots on the horizon, along with a number of other test varietals. One of its star attractions, the cabernet franc rosé, has received the most acclaim since the winery's opening in 2011. Awarded a bronze metal for its crisp, clean, strawberry-infused taste, the rosé is difficult to keep in stock.

Top and Bottom: Three estate best-sellers, Unoaked Chardonnay, Cabernet Merlot, and Riesling, have received surprising acclaim from wine lovers and aficionados alike. Whether guests prefer several flights or one full pour, wines are sure to be enjoyed in an unforgettable locale, engaging all the senses.

Facing Page: Sleek, contemporary, and artsy, the tasting room invites visitors into a sophisticated setting.
Photographs by Steven Elphick

Located on Eden-like terrain, the land is home to an abundance of natural resources. Teeming with wildlife, the green scenery nurtures singing ponds, buzzing honeycombs, and birds of prey. An apple and peach orchard add to the property's charm and further demonstrate the soil's wholesome consistency. Future plans for the always-evolving property include a sustainable garden of garlic and potatoes as well as the addition of a greenland—containing thousands of trees—and a wetland commissioned by Ducks Unlimited.

Guardians of the vines, birds of prey soar above the vineyard stalking the lesser of their kind for food. Hawks are especially prevalent above the estate—the Cooper Hawk specifically—which is the inspiration behind the winery's name and silhouetted label. Essentially consuming the birds that consume the grapes, they are well-respected allies and nature's pest control for the crops.

Top and Bottom: One of many test-grape varieties in the vineyard, Proprietors Reserve is expected to receive as much admiration from connoisseurs as the much-loved riesling grapes do.

Facing Page Top: The modern winery was designed to enhance the vineyard's natural beauty, showcasing its leafy vines through expansive windows.

Facing Page Bottom: An estate supremely aware of its carbon footprint, the winery has installed solar panels to provide energy for the winery, which also participates in tree planting and habitat preservation.
Photographs by Steven Elphick

Keeping with sustainable practices, the winery harnesses energy by way of solar panels and conserves it using updated technology such as in-floor heating. Simple and purposeful, its utilitarian structure is made of sawed red cedar and ruffian pine, which harmonizes well with the wonderland outside.

Nature-lovers and wine-lovers are able to enjoy the family friendly atmosphere found at Cooper's Hawk. Bottle in hand, patrons are encouraged to bring a blanket and seek out the perfect spot for a total experience. With a property garden, home-grown culinary creations are sure to increase and the O'Briens look forward to crafting flavorful plates that complement their impressive vintages.

Top: The O'Briens appreciate and encourage family interaction at the estate. Extensive areas for running and playing are available to children while parents decompress with a glass of wine.

Middle: When Tom is not in the winery or tasting room, he can often be found maintaining the vineyard and estate grounds.

Bottom: Owners Tom and Katy, along with their son Michael, welcome visitors to the tasting room and state-of-the-art facility.

Facing Page: Bonfires are an alfresco delight in the summer months. Guests gather around with their favorite glass and enjoy a feeling of euphoria that an azure sky sprinkled with brilliant stars and an open fire can provide.
Photographs by Steven Elphick

Cabernet Merlot
Pair with braised beef ribs, potatoes au gratin, and sautéed spinach.

Chardonnay
Pair with smoked salmon in a creamy white wine reduction sauce over seasoned wild rice.

Cabernet Franc Rosé
Pair with lightly breaded and golden-fried oysters, clams, and shrimp.

Riesling
Pair with an antipasti plate of assorted cheeses such as Jarlesburg, Gruyere, and Appenzeller.

Tastings
Open daily, year-round

Pelee Island Winery

Kingsville

Positioned approximately 12 miles south of Canada's mainland and within the great Lake Erie, Pelee Island is the southernmost point of Canada's territory, maintaining a permanent population of up to 300, with the exception of tourist-filled summer months. Not only is it a picturesque location for coastal living, the island is a well known wine-producing region dating back to the 1800s. The tradition of crafting award-winning wines, on both a national and international level, has continued on the island since receiving an internationally recognized medal in Paris in 1878.

Pelee Island is home to the first estate winery in Canada; Vin Villa was founded in the 1860s and still stands today. With the longest growing season in Canada, wineries like Pelee Island Winery in Kingsville have a natural advantage when it comes to harvesting vitis vinifera such as chardonnay, gewürztraminer, riesling, sauvignon blanc, pinot noir, cabernet sauvignon, cabernet franc, and several others. While the extended growing season offers an edge, it is only one contributing factor of many that make these wines so savory.

The island's terroir—made of toledo soil and brookstone clay over a limestone base—is also a defining factor when it comes to the singular character of the fruit. Found on 550-plus acres of vines, the grapes flourish in an ideal climate of 800 millimeters of rainfall each year. Sunning under an average of 1,591 heat units, the grapes are allowed to reach full maturity, allowing for robust flavors.

Top: The Pelee Island Lighthouse is located on the northern tip of Pelee Island at Lighthouse Point.
Photograph courtesy of Pelee Island Winery

Middle: Grapes ripen on the vine.
Photograph by Steven Elphick

Bottom: The Pelee Island wine pavilion and vineyards.
Photograph courtesy of Pelee Island Winery

Facing Page: Pelee Island is an oasis of green surrounded by the blue waters of Lake Erie.
Photograph by Steven Elphick

Pelee Island Winery has been owned by the Trapp-Dries family since the 1980s. The family's grape growing and winemaking history dates back to the early 17th century in Germany's Rhine Valley. Winemaster Martin Janz continues to apply Germanic techniques to the estate's world-quality wines, which have been recognized in prestigious competitions such as Vinexpo in France, Vinitaly in Verona, and the International Wine and Spirits Competition in London. Martin attended the Rheingau Institute of Winemaking, and upon graduation in 1996 he moved to Canada to begin a career as winemaker to Walter Schmoranz, one of Canada's winemaking pioneers. When he joined Pelee in 1985, it was an adolescent; less than a decade old. Since then, he has vaulted Pelee onto the world stage, most notably for a 2002 cabernet franc icewine, the winner of the Citadelle de France gold medal.

Above: The Pelee Island Winery production facilities have been located on the mainland in Kingsville since 1982.

Right: A bottle each of Pelee Island Winery Chardonnay Barrique and Meritage.

Facing Page Bottom Left: President and winemaster Walter Schmoranz, wine master Martin Janz, and winemaker Tim Charisse comprise the Pelee Island Winery team.

Facing Page Bottom Right: Stoneware tanks are used to hold raw distillate from the distillery.
Photographs by Steven Elphick

Although the winery was incorporated in 1979, the Kingsville location was not established until 1982, with the wine pavilion on the island following in 1991. Perfect for a summer day trip, the pavilion and wine garden overlook the lake and are often a hotspot for warm weather activities. The winery is popular year-round, playing host to special events and weddings on a regular basis. It requires an entire day, or even a weekend, to properly explore the exclusive 10,000-acre natural treasure that is Pelee Island. Boasting thousands of plants and wildlife within the Carolinian habitat, the surroundings are ideal for birdwatchers, hikers, and cyclists alike.

Since 1982, production facilities have been located on the mainland in Kingsville, a mere 30 minutes from the Ambassador Bridge between Windsor and Detroit, Michigan. Visitors are invited to explore an extensive retail store and journey along a comprehensive tour of the winemaking establishment. On the island, an equally exciting experience awaits, where guests can tour, taste, and enjoy a barbecued lunch overlooking Lake Erie from the wine pavilion's thriving garden.

Top: The winery has a retail store and gift boutique.
Photograph by Steven Elphick

Middle and Facing Page: The tasting room at the Kingsville location is European in style.
Photographs by Steven Elphick

Bottom: The barrel room holds precious vintages.
Photograph courtesy of Pelee Island Winery

Pinot Grigio
Pair with grilled perch or pickerel drizzled with chermoula sauce over tomato and green pepper pilaf.

Cabernet Franc
Pair with roasted and butterflied leg of lamb seasoned with garlic and thyme.

Alvar Pinot Noir
Pair with pinot noir-braised beef shanks served with sautéed mushrooms and basil mashed potatoes.

Tastings
Open to the public daily, year-round

Viewpointe Estate Winery

Harrow

I f a winery reflects the personality of its owners, then John, Steve, and Jean Fancsy must be one warm and welcoming family. Their Viewpointe Estate Winery, which opened for business in 2006, is one of the most relaxing destinations on the north shore of Lake Erie. Every wine in the cellar is governed by a no-rush, no-fuss policy. Every window in the estate's tasting room frames a picture-perfect view of the lake. And every afternoon in the spring, summer, and fall finds Viewpointe with a patio full of laid-back, contented guests enjoying fine regional cuisine paired with award-winning wines.

The choice of location on a bluff on Lake Erie's north shore and attention to sustainable practices speak of a family that cares deeply about both hospitality and keeping it local. The winery may be one of the newer operations in the appellation, but you would never know from the Old World-style wines and Victorian-era inspired architecture. Modeled after the historic Mettawas Hotel and Casino, built by Hiram Walker in nearby Kingsville, Ontario, in 1889, Viewpointe's main building houses a tasting room, a professional kitchen large enough to hold popular cooking classes, and well-appointed rooms for hosting events. Building materials were thoughtfully sourced regionally and locally; the natural stone is pure Ontario. The white oak and hickory woods were sourced from the surrounding Carolinian forests.

Top: High Pointe Syrah, Balance Pointe Cabernet-Merlot Blend, and Auxerrois.

Bottom: Delicious food is available to Viewpointe visitors.

Facing Page: The Erie Room provides an incredible view of the lake.
Photographs by Steven Elphick

Guests are treated as family. Menus for lunches, dinners, and all events are created to pair exquisitely with the wines, as well as showcase the abundant local, fresh "bounty of the county." Guided tours take visitors through the vineyards, some of the winemaking areas, and the underground barrel room, as well as throughout the various event spaces. Tours finish up on the patio, with guests nibbling on something local and tasty while sipping some beautifully crafted wine, enjoying the peace and beauty of the lakeside setting.

Many of these same wine-loving regulars return for the popular local event Explore the Shore: Discover County Road 50. This weekend event takes place in late July, when local businesses along historic County Road 50 showcase the best the region has to offer. Tourists flock to this area to taste wine, sample food, learn, and enjoy the beautiful area and all it has to offer.

Viewpointe is all about growth and knowledge. It is a satellite campus of the Canadian Food and Wine Institute, offering a two-year Master Taster Certificate with an in-depth curriculum covering multiple aspects of all things wine.

Top: The spacious patio is perfect for special events.

Middle: Masonry protects Viewpointe and its patrons from the elements.

Bottom: The Colchester Room, a quiet space within the building, serves as the location for the Master Taster Certification program.

Facing Page Top: Viewpointe Estate Winery's east elevation.

Facing Page Bottom: Fine vintages age in barrels in the cellar.
Photographs by Steven Elphick

As an engineer, John keeps his feet firmly planted in the science of the business. Realizing how well the Auxerrois grape does in the vineyard and despite its typical use as a blending component, he took a chance and bottled Auxerrois as a wine on its own. This wine is a perennial favorite now, and customers eagerly await upcoming vintage releases.

In the pursuit of sustainability, John and Steve have been pioneers in the advancement of experimental grapes. Ever since the winery's inception, they have been working on the development of sustainable grape varieties, and have been successful to the point of winning an Agri-Food Innovation Ontario award in 2009 for a series of grape varietals known as HG, or Harrow Grafted.

These are the kinds of calculated risks John, Steve, and Jean like to take. Truth be told, the last thing they want to do is chase trends. Instead, they are most interested in being honest and truthful and letting the grapes express themselves. To ensure the grapes have the perfect atmosphere in which to do this seemingly basic—yet very complicated—job, Viewpointe invests heavily in fine oak barrels and intervenes with the grapes as little as possible. The owners have found that if you make wine truthfully, the result will be more timeless than any trend.

Above Left: John Fancsy is president, winemaker, and co-owner of Viewpointe Estate Winery.

Above Right: Colchester Cuvée is crafted from sustainable grape varieties.

Facing Page: Viewpointe's Winery Shoppe is a requisite stop for visitors.
Photographs by Steven Elphick

Sauvignon Blanc
Fantastic with marinated goat cheese, roasted red pepper, and sundried tomato.

Pinot Grigio
Delicious alongside citrus-honey glazed chicken with an Auxerrois reduction.

Cabernet Franc
Serve with spinach and ricotta-stuffed ravioli and tomato-basil sauce.

Pinot Noir
Pairs well with mushroom, Parmesan, and leek bread pudding.

Tastings
Open to the public year-round, tours by appointment

Georgian Hills Vineyards, page 282

Coffin Ridge Winery, page 278

Magnotta Winery, page 286

Willow Springs Winery, page 294

Coffin Ridge Winery

Annan

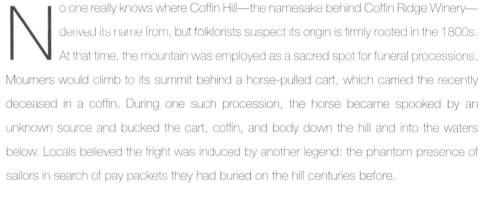

N o one really knows where Coffin Hill—the namesake behind Coffin Ridge Winery—derived its name from, but folklorists suspect its origin is firmly rooted in the 1800s. At that time, the mountain was employed as a sacred spot for funeral processions. Mourners would climb to its summit behind a horse-pulled cart, which carried the recently deceased in a coffin. During one such procession, the horse became spooked by an unknown source and bucked the cart, coffin, and body down the hill and into the waters below. Locals believed the fright was induced by another legend: the phantom presence of sailors in search of pay packets they had buried on the hill centuries before.

Neil and Gwen Lamont, owners of Coffin Ridge Winery, began their grape growing journey in 1999, in the shadow of that hill. The vineyards were the brainchild of Neil, whose curiosity was picqued by the abundance of wild grapes growing in the area; in order to satisfy his curiosity, Neil planted 200 vines around the house, which surprisingly survived the harsh Grey County winter. The results encouraged Neil to plant even more vines, which he did with the help of friends and family.

Today, nestled in the Niagara Escarpment, Coffin Ridge Winery tempts guests to "experience the mystery of wine" while overlooking the beautiful 25-acre vineyard and azure waters of Georgian Bay. The vineyard is carefully tended to using sustainable viticulture practices, which results in healthy grapes and great wines. Coffin Ridge is Grey County's first winery, producing artisanal wines that are made from cutting-edge hybrid grapes including marquette, l'acadie blanc, Geisenheim, baco noir, and maréchal foch.

Top: Hand-made pine gift boxes further the estate's macabre theme, as they take the shape of a tiny coffin. Crafted by local artisan Chuck Merrill, the box neatly displays a bottle of signature wine: Back From the Dead Red.

Bottom: The winery's black façade is accented by blood-red trim, creating a dramatic first impression.

Facing Page: The vineyards at Coffin Ridge are other-worldly at sunset, punctuated by the legendary Coffin Hill just beyond. *Photographs by Steven Elphick*

With the help of a knowledgeable team, Coffin Ridge produces award-winning wines. General manager Michael Todd—fondly known as the grape slayer—is said to be the driving force behind the estate. He gently nurtures the vines until harvest, when he ushers the beloved grapes into their transformation. The process continues in the winery, where talented winemaker Steve Byfield brings each bottle to new life. They are then labeled and sold by tasting room manager Willow Todd, who finishes the artful ritual. Believing that good wine enhances the celebratory nature of food and relationships, the estate encourages visitors to come by, choose a wine, and indulge in a vintner's plate of perfectly paired cheeses while admiring the view. Who knows? Visits after sunset may include eerie figures on Coffin Hill, digging in search of their misplaced money.

Above Left: Coffin Ridge is successfully run by two families: proprietors Neil and Gwen Lamont, along with Willow and Michael Todd.

Above Right: The sophisticated tasting room features a handcrafted walnut tasting bar, where patrons can enjoy complimentary flights of wines.

Left: The vintner's plate is an assortment of locally crafted cheeses, pâté, seasonal fruit, and fresh-baked bread. It is perfect paired with an artisanal glass of wine.

Facing Page: Beautiful decks and lawns offer ample seating for views of the vineyards and the spectacular Georgian Bay.
Photographs by Steven Elphick

Into the Light White
Pair with Georgian Bay smoked trout pâté, curried meats, or savory shortbread.

Back From the Dead Red
Pair with Asian orange beef, spicy ribs, or dark chocolate.

Resurrection Rosé
Pair with bocconcini salad or light pasta.

Sparkling Pear
Pair with savory blue cheese cake or pear and walnut salad.

Tastings
Open to the public daily

Georgian Hills Vineyards

The Blue Mountains

Legend has it that the great Lake Huron was once under the guard of a god named Kitchikewana, who was known to harbor a fiery temper. In efforts to soothe him, his tribe decided to seek out a wife for their god and arranged a party for interested suitors. Once Kitchikewana was introduced to a woman named Wanakita, he fell deeply in love, only to discover that she was already engaged. Full of rage, Kitchikewana grabbed a ball of earth and tossed it into the Great Lakes. The indentations of his fingers can still be seen today in the form the five bays, one of which is Georgian Bay.

Located on the hillside overlooking Georgian Bay, Ardiel Acres Vineyards and Georgian Hills Vineyards thrive in clay loam soil rich with sediments left by glacial bodies from the last great Ice Age. Planted in 2003 and 2007 respectively, the vineyards take advantage of concentrated sun exposure to the south and west and north-flowing thermal air to keep the vines relatively sheltered from harsh elements. The not-yet-recognized region of Georgian Bay has similar characteristics to that of the Niagara Peninsula appellation, with slight nuances. The idyllic environment benefits the production of white varietals boasting vibrant citrus and stone fruit notes and reds that reflect remarkable berry flavors indicative of the terroir. Additionally, certain grapes are allowed to hang on the vine until early winter in order to freeze and are used to make sensational winter wines like Vidal Frozen on the Vine, a gold medal winner and best-seller for the estate.

Top: Some of Georgian Hills' fine wines include VQA-certified selections such as pinot noir, riesling, gewürztraminer, and other sweet winter wines like Vidal Frozen on the Vine and Ida Red Frozen to the Core.

Bottom: Partners John Ardiel, Robert Ketchin, and Murray Puddicombe, with adored dog Buster, contribute their personal talents to the winery's continual success.

Facing Page: Spectacular views of the majestic Blue Mountains can be seen from five acres of vines hidden among the orchards.
Photographs by Steven Elphick

Modern-day pioneers Murray Puddicombe, John Ardiel, and Robert Ketchin purchased an old apple orchard and repurposed it for growing grapes. Fourth-generation grape grower and previous founder of Stoney Ridge Winery, Murray has an intimate understanding of the culture. Likewise, John of Beaver Valley is a fourth-generation grower—of apples, ironically—and president of Bay Growers. Their cumulative experience in growing, paired with the business savvy of marketing maven and fellow partner Robert, has afforded Georgian Hills a practical dream team from planting the vines to designing the label.

Lindsay Puddicombe, Murray's daughter, is a fifth-generation winemaker and the artist behind the 10-plus VQA white, red, rosé, and sweet winter wines made at the estate.

A refinished cow barn original to the property has proven to be the perfect winery, authentic to the history of the land. Similarly, a restored bunkhouse acts as a retail store stocked full of delicious vintages for every palate.

Top: Twelve acres of verdant vines make up Georgian Hills Vineyards, located in the heart of Beaver Valley and surrounded by the escarpment.
Photograph by Steven Elphick

Middle: Ideal for growing grapes as well as apples, the bay's climate is perfect for making Ida Red Frozen to the Core iced apple wine.
Photograph by Steven Elphick

Bottom: The winter harvest is celebrated with friends and neighbors who help pick the varietal vidal blanc in order to make the Frozen on the Vine specialty.
Photograph by Julie Card

Facing Page: The pristine bay is located only minutes away from the vineyard. Glassy waters, soft sand, and nautical peace awaits at the end of a brief commute.
Photograph by Steven Elphick

Seyval Blanc
Pair with a spinach salad with Cape Vessey goat cheese and McIntosh apples tossed in citrus vinaigrette with walnuts.

Gamay Rosé
Enjoy with Kolapore Springs smoked trout over wild rice with almond-encrusted green beans.

Marechal Foch
Sip with Ontario lamb burgers garnished with caramelized onions and arugula.

Tastings
Open to the public Wednesday through Sunday, year-round

GEORGIAN HILLS
VINEYARDS

Magnotta Winery
Vaughan/Beamsville

I n 1990, when Rossana Magnotta's husband Gabe, a passionate outdoorsman with an entrepreneurial spirit, floated the idea of starting a family winery, it had never occurred to Rossana that she might have a career outside of the medical laboratory. She had been an avid home winemaker since her youth before pursuing a career in diagnostic medicine, so when Gabe brought up his idea, Rossana, who was taking a break to raise their children, was intrigued. Gabe was drawn to the idea of establishing a family business, but he also knew that he didn't have the skill set to do it alone. After much conversation, establishing a winery that would bear the family name and someday be handed down to their three children struck a chord with the duo. They realized that Rossana's diagnostic leanings combined with Gabe's business savvy could result in something that was a perfect match for both their talents.

They started on a shoestring budget, pouring nearly every cent into purchasing the former Charal Winery in Blenheim and establishing a modest winemaking venture with a home winemaking component. Rossana realized that whether you're testing for sugar levels in blood or wine, the chemistry is the same, so she took on the role of onsite chemist, analyzing and batch-testing the winery's commercial wines.

When it came time to bottle their first run, there wasn't any money left to hire a graphic artist to design labels. Never ones to give up on a challenge, they realized that their personal art collection would make the perfect template for a series of artistic labels. They began contacting the local artists whose paintings hung throughout their own home, asking them to allow their work to be used on the new winery's bottles. Many were personal friends who were thrilled to give their permission, and Magnotta Winery's signature art labels were born.

Top: A folk art, hand-painted barrel by Gilles Pelletier is part of Magnotta's extensive art collection that is displayed throughout the winery.

Bottom: Cathedral ceilings at the Vaughan winery help showcase original works of art that have inspired the winery's label designs.

Facing Page: The Vaughan winery is a 75,000-square-foot architectural triumph that features a state-of-the-art winemaking and bottling facility, temperature-controlled underground cellar, microbrewery, and copper pot distillery.
Photographs by Steven Elphick

Today many of the 400 paintings from Magnotta's impressive collection that have been used for its labels hang throughout the winery's bright, teak common spaces. Customers who may not recall the name of their favorite wine will always remember the label, asking for the cabernet with the horse on it or the Meritage with the Picasso-esque woman playing the violin. And if the wine is new to them, they can usually glean its personality—fun, serious, moody, or cool—from the art Rossana has chosen to accompany it. As opposed to other wineries that may lease the rights to the art they use, Rossana purchases the paintings outright, adding them to the winery's ever-expanding gallery. As a result, up-and-coming artists line up for the honor of being showcased on a label. The alliance with Magnotta provides them with instant international visibility and name recognition, as each artist's name is included on every label.

Left: Rossana Di Zio Magnotta is the president and CEO. Two of Rossana's greatest passions are continuing to grow her successful winery and competing in international skeet events.
Photograph by Steven Elphick

As the third-largest winery in Ontario, Magnotta produces over 180 award-winning wines in every category, from VQA premium wines and icewines to sparkling and dessert wines, and is the proud creator of the world's first sparkling icewine, Sparkling Ice™. The winery is also especially proud of its big, full-throttle reds. These Bordeaux-style blends, such as Magnotta's Enotrium Gran Riserva, are carefully crafted using Amarone-style techniques. Magnotta was the first winery in Canada to vinify the finest, hand-harvested Ontario grapes using the same air drying methods employed in Italy. This traditional process produces wines of exceptional character, complexity, and longevity. By showcasing her world-class reds and successfully going up against California, Bordeaux, and Chilean reds, Rossana is helping to break down the misconception that cool-climate Ontario reds are thin and light.

What started with that initial land purchase in Blenheim expanded into four properties stretching from Niagara-on-the-Lake to Beamsville. The 26-acre Beamsville Bench property benefits from rich limestone, loam soil, and a gentle slope, while the flatter 120-acre Merritt Road location benefits from more moderate temperatures. The property stretches all the way from the QEW to Lake Ontario and has produced some of the best wines the company has ever decanted.

Above: Magnotta's premium wines have won prestigious competitions in Europe—including France and Italy—as well as competitions at home in Canada.

Right: Magnotta's retail stores are warm, spacious, and offer over 180 world-class wines in every category that can be tasted at each of the stores' complimentary tasting bars.

Facing Page Top: The underground, temperature-controlled cellar at Vaughan features European chandeliers and an elegant 40-foot oak tasting table.

Facing Page Bottom: Traditional natural corks allow Magnotta's premium wines to age to perfection over a long period of time.
Photographs by Steven Elphick

The clay and silt soil on the two Niagara-on-the-Lake properties is famous for producing excellent chardonnay and pinot noir. Today the combined acreage sits at close to 200 acres. Rossana also contracts grapes from local growers. However, the grapes for the company's top vintages always come from one of the Magnotta properties.

Sadly, in 2009, the Magnotta family lost Gabe to Lyme disease. While the loss has been profound and challenging, the events surrounding Gabe's death brought Rossana full circle, focusing her interests once again on the diagnostic medical world that means so much to her. In honor of Gabe's struggle, she established a campaign to educate people about the devastation of Lyme disease. As a director of the Canadian Lyme Disease Foundation, she has made impressive inroads, including progress toward creating the first facility for research, testing, and treatment of Lyme and tick-borne diseases in Canada.

Although Rossana's soul lies in medical activism and the founding of the G. Magnotta Foundation for Vector-Borne Diseases, her heart continues to be the pulse behind the winery. The dream she had with Gabe over 20 years ago is unfolding as they imagined. With Rossana continuing to taste every wine before it goes into the bottle and their grown children, Tommaso, Joseph, and Alessia, participating in all aspects of winery operations, the Magnotta legacy is a picture of personal success worthy of a label of its own.

Above Left: Magnotta's Cabernet Sauvignon and Sauvignon Blanc Special Reserve VQA wines help spread awareness of Lyme disease in Canada. A portion of the proceeds goes to CanLyme.

Above Right: A winemaker for over 20 years, Rossana works closely with her enologists and personally tastes every wine under development at Magnotta.

Facing Page: Hand-painted by local artist Irmtraud, the wall leading to the underground cellar is a fitting greeting to wine aficionados descending for a wine tasting event.
Photographs by Steven Elphick

Enotrium Gran Riserva VQA
Perfect with steak, venison, and wild game.

Vidal Sparkling Ice Merritt Road Limited Edition VQA
Absolutely luscious with intensely flavored cheeses,
pâtés, and cheesecake.

Pinot Gris Special Reserve VQA
Superb with scallops, lobster tail, and mild creamy cheeses.

Shiraz Limited Edition VQA
Exquisite with lamb, duck, quail, and a variety of game meats.

Tastings
Open daily, year-round

MAGNOTTA
The Award Winning Winery

Willow Springs Winery

Stouffville

Willow Springs Winery, a quaint, family-owned winery in Stouffville, aims to provide its visitors with fine wine and distinctive event planning. A typical day at the winery could encompass the creation of award-winning wines in its traditional facilities while outside a wedding party basks in the shade of willow trees and the shimmering reflections of the pond. After being told that a vineyard just could not flourish on the land, founder and winemaker Mario Testa planted a test plot of vines, hoping to start a crop of grapes as a part-time hobby on the Testa family farm, which dates to the 1960s. Much to everyone's surprise, what started out as a hobby quickly grew into a full-time career for the Testa family. The winery became fully operational in 2001.

Willow Springs, both a winery and an event destination, produces distinctive varietals: chardonnay, sauvignon blanc, merlot, Meritage, cabernet franc, baco noir, rosé, and icewines. The 11-acre vineyard situated atop the Oak Ridges Moraine—one of Ontario's last remaining continuous green corridors and home to more than 60 glacial waterways—is one of the coldest vineyards in the world. Willow Springs possesses a delightfully rural appeal while still being a part of the Greater Toronto Area; it has all the comforts of the country without the remote location.

Top: Winemaking in the olden days is honored at the winery.

Bottom: Only fresh grapes are used for the Willow Springs brand.

Facing Page: Guest are encouraged to take time to reflect at the pond.
Photographs by Steven Elphick

The villas and winery facility feature rustic architecture with exposed wood beam ceilings and wrought iron lighting. Décor for events is casual chic, utilizing items from the wine industry in the design, such as a grapevine gazebo or wine barrels used as aisle markers for weddings. The wine boutique features an uncluttered retail space where the focus is truly upon the wines produced at Willow Springs. The buildings and grounds are warm and inviting. Whether attending corporate or private events, guests are able to experience all aspects of the winemaking business at Willow Springs.

With a team consisting of marketing manager Sheridan Huang, event manager Michael Cheung, wedding and event consultant Rhonda Robinson, and marketing and sales coordinator Bo Li, Willow Springs offers inclusive wedding and event packages for all who crave the winery experience. It also hosts holiday-centric events at Easter, Mother's Day, Father's Day, and Christmas and offers tours and tastings to the public.

Top and Middle Left: The wine boutique brings a touch of country elegance to any event.

Middle Right: Founder and winemaker Mario Testa.

Bottom: The rustic winemaker's pavilion is perfect for any occasion.

Facing Page: Willow Springs Winery is minutes away from the city but miles away from ordinary.
Photographs by Steven Elphick

Baco Noir
Couples exquisitely with heavier-style meals such as Italian pasta or hamburgers.

Moraine White
Pairs delightfully with seafood and spicy Asian cuisine such as sushi, crab cakes, or spicy noodles.

Meritage
Flawless with smoky barbecue-style meals or hearty red meat.

Vidal Icewine
Complements any fruit-based dessert or strong and rich cheeses such as blue cheese or aged Cheddar.

Tastings
Open to the public daily

The Cheese Gallery, page 308

Humble Bread, page 316

The Waring House, page 334

Wine Awakenings, page 338

13th Street Bakery
and Marketplace

St. Catharines

The visitors to 13th Street Winery do not have to wander far to find artisan cheese, soups, gourmet flatbread, and other fine eats to pair with wines by the glass. Steps away from the tasting room, the 13th Street Bakery and Marketplace inhabits a renovated barn and wafts rich aromas—from fresh, locally grown, in-season fruits and vegetables to baked goods, gourmet creations, and handcrafted products like fine teas and soaps—toward the winery doors. The companies are perfectly coupled; a fantastical setting where good food follows good wine amid pristine countryside.

A major supplier of goods to the marketplace and bakery, and a St. Catharines institution since 1908, is Whitty Farms. Believing that those who eat well will live well, the farm is a local mainstay that cultivates relationships with the community through fun festivities and fresh options. Its commitment to agricultural innovation and ongoing research illustrates an authentic desire to improve product integrity for optimum consumption. As a sister company to the winery, the farm is owned and operated by the same family who oversees all of 13th Street's endeavors, which explains the farm's flavor-packed presence at the neighboring marketplace. Fresh and seasonal fruits from Niagara's pure terroir are truly nature's candy, some of which become pantry staples such as jams, jellies, and preserves, or baked goods made onsite by Joanne Lenz, Karen's sister. Affectionately known as Jo Pie, Joanne crafts the fruit into hundreds of tarts, fruit pies, cookies, and cakes baked for sweet-tooth satisfaction.

Top: Fresh fruit from the fields is crafted into jams and jellies that can be enjoyed year-round.

Middle: Peach pie is one of the many seasonal fruit pies available at 13th Street Bakery and Marketplace.

Bottom: The wine shop and bakery are located just steps from the 13th Street Winery property.

Facing Page: A bountiful harvest doesn't have to be limited to wine.
Photographs by Steven Elphick

Temptation continues as foodies maneuver through an explosion of colors, textures, and aromas. From flatbread pizzas to artichoke tapenade and sweet basil pesto oil, creamy Brie cheese topped with sweet cranberry and orange liqueur to apricot jalapeño jelly—all have been known to ignite bursts of excitement. Smoky garlic white bean soup and peach salsa with garlic from Ontario await discovery by visitors.

While the marketplace and bakery offer authentic Niagara products year-round, certain creations are available by season and crafted in limited supply. Non-perishable items such as jewelry, books, kitchen gadgets, scarves, and other fun merchandise fit easily into carry-on bags, while maple syrup, honey, salsas, chutneys, tapenades, and oils may require special wrapping for the journey home.

Above and Facing Page: The café offers a casual garden setting in which to enjoy a glass of wine with a slice of gourmet flatbread pizza or a cup of coffee to accompany a famous butter tart.

Right: Karen Whitty is the general manager of 13th Street Winery and 13th Street Bakery. She co-owns the business with her husband Doug, plus friends June and John Mann.
Photographs by Steven Elphick

Cheese Boutique

Toronto

In 1968, Hysen and Stella Pristine immigrated to Toronto with little more than the clothes on their backs and the dream of starting a business. He was from Albania, she from Naples, and Ontario presented the opportunity to see their dream realized. In 1970, Cheese Boutique's original location was opened in Toronto as a shop that occupied a little over 600 square feet of real estate. Growing into a gourmet must-visit store and eventually outgrowing the tiny premises, Cheese Boutique moved into a new home in a former sausage factory on an industrial strip where it is now able to offer more than 500 types of cheeses from all over the world.

Patrons are encouraged to sample an array of exotic cheeses from far-flung reaches of the globe. If food and wine pairing is a need, staff members are more than willing—and quite qualified—to help. Some hold sommelier certifications, and others have simply been in the business long enough to age their cheese experience into expertise. Fatos, the second generation of Pristines, has been honored as a Knight of the Order of Agricultural Merit by the government of France, and both he and his son Afrim have been named Chevalier by the Confrérie des Chevaliers du Taste Fromage de France, organizations that recognize excellence in their industry.

The store also offers alternative wedding cakes for couples who would prefer wheels of cheese to sugary confections. Afrim, the face of Cheese Boutique's third generation, meets with couples to design, taste test, and construct elegant "wedding cakes" of cheese for the big day.

Top: The front gates of Cheese Boutique lead to the gelateria.

Bottom: The exclusive cheese cave features a 950-pound auricchio provolone imported from Italy. Only two of these cheeses are made each year.

Facing Page: The shop offers a wide selection of exotic cheese including brilliant savarin, affienato, and Roquefort blue.
Photographs by Steven Elphick

The cosmopolitan shop embraces global products of high quality; members of the Pristine family travel around the world selecting the very best products to stock in the shop—everything from world-class cheese to foie gras, imported olives, jams and jellies, fresh-baked goods, and produce. Since 2003, Cheese Boutique has hosted Festival of Chefs, a celebration of food and wine. At the annual event, top chefs prepare dishes of their choice in the store, while four of Ontario's top wineries pair their wines with the cuisine for a minimal donation that benefits a local charity.

While it sounds glamorous, Cheese Boutique is living proof that thriving businesses are those which have been cultivated, loved, and endlessly pursued. Fatos and his wife Modesta have worked well past the conventional retirement age and they have instilled the ethics of hard work and dedication in their four sons Agim, Ilir, Afrim, and Arian, and two daughters-in-law Melissa and Sophia, all of whom work in essential roles for the business. Combining this sense of strong family ties and philanthropy with Old World personal service, Cheese Boutique has become a stop for many Canadians wishing to experience culinary delights.

Top: Cheese Boutique's front entrance has a welcoming ambience.

Bottom: Seated in the center of the pasta room is Fatos Pristine along with three of his four sons: Ilir, Arian, and Agim.

Facing Page Top Left: Cheese Boutique carries a selection of fresh pastries, baked daily.

Facing Page Top Right: Many delectable cheeses age to perfection in the cheese vault.

Facing Page Bottom: The selection of pasta rivals those found in Italy.
Photographs by Steven Elphick

The Cheese Gallery

Thornbury

While on a blistery winter hike along the Niagara Escarpment, Casey Thomson began throwing business ideas around with some girlfriends. Casey looked for a new challenge, and wanted to bring the harbor town of Thornbury a market stocked with goods from local producers and artisans, all in a charmingly sophisticated venue. From that day on the beautiful escarpment, The Cheese Gallery was born.

Moving from Toronto to Thornbury, Casey found that the area needed more gourmet food choices—something beyond the local grocery store. So Casey took her love of cheese, wine, chocolate, and fresh bread to new heights. In the ultimate leap of faith—after extensive research, of course—Casey opened The Cheese Gallery in June of 2010. Just one year later, the shop was awarded Entrepreneur of the Year by the Blue Mountains Chamber of Commerce, an award based on nominations and votes from chamber members and local residents.

As one of the only cheese shops in Ontario with a liquor license, The Cheese Gallery is privileged to partner with many of the wineries that dot the Ontario landscape. Visitors to the shop are encouraged to sit at the bar—made from locally sourced Georgian Bay rocks—sip 2010 Seyval Blanc from Georgian Hills Vineyards or sample Coffin Ridge Winery's 2010 Sparkling Pear wine, while munching on cheese plates stocked with locally produced goodies. Casey, her husband Brendan, daughters McKenzie and Kennedy, and other team members who resemble good friends rather than employees, want patrons to feel free to sample, poke, and browse the shop's shelves, or simply sit in a cozy corner sipping wine.

Top: Casey Thompson, founder and owner of The Cheese Gallery, encourages visitors to relax at the wine and tea bar.

Bottom: Mature Cheddar with single malt whisky from Scotland, four-year-old Thunder Oak Gouda from Ontario, three-year-old raw milk Parmesan from Italy, and Roquefort from France paired with Coffin Ridge Winery's Back from the Dead Red wine served on a handmade cheeseboard make a perfect presentation.

Facing Page: The Cheese Gallery building, circa 1887, was a men's tailor shop for more than 100 years. Today it welcomes locals and visitors alike to experience "edible art."
Photographs by Steven Elphick

One of the founding members of the Apple Pie Trail, a delicious journey that stretches along the coast of the Georgian Bay, The Cheese Gallery welcomes travelers with apple cider, apple cheese boards, and apple-smoked Cheddar. Also featured are "edible art" pieces—objects created by local artisans that center on an edible theme, whether they be French butter dishes and cutting boards or hand-blown martini glasses and handmade peppermills. The Cheese Gallery features a wide array of Ontario cheeses. Many of the cheeses available in the shop are raw milk cheeses, made in the European fashion, but the shop also presents cheese from France, Scotland, and Wisconsin. These are all accentuated by the shop's environment: a centuries-old brick building with a cheery, French-inspired façade and a chic European interior.

Top: Local food artisans produce many of the offerings at The Cheese Gallery for visitors to enjoy when they drop by for a sip or a nibble.

Middle: There's no rush in Thornbury, and a cozy gathering place with comfy chairs is the perfect place to relax. Guests of the shop may enjoy a hot cup of tea and a freshly baked croissant paired with local jam.

Bottom: The Cheese Gallery carries over 100 cheese types from around the world, many of which are produced in Canada.

Facing Page: The Georgian Bay wine and tea bar is a great place to share a cheese tasting plate or a gourmet grilled cheese with a glass of wine.
Photographs by Steven Elphick

H2O2 Wine Cellar Design

Toronto

H2O2 Wine Cellar Design was formed in January of 2010 by an avid collector and fellow consumer who was passionate about the proper storage of wine and the imperative, but largely overlooked, education of its owners. After discovering that many collectors were not storing their beloved vintages in controlled environments—most likely due to high-market-cost designs—Wilfred Yu abandoned a career in logistics and embraced a plan to fill the industry need. As the drinking, collecting, and storage of wine dates back thousands of years, so does the proper way to care for it. Whether it is a wine rack, walk-in wine room, or state-of-the-art cellar with humidity-controlled air conditioning beneath the ground, the design is imperative to the life of the wine and enjoyment of the collector.

Customizing cellars for individuals as well as restaurants, H2O2's team has been involved in numerous projects throughout Toronto and its surrounding areas. From 1,000-plus bottle walk-ins to an astounding inclusion within a 25,000-square-foot mansion, the team can covert almost any space into a customized cellar. Experience working with custom home builders, architects, and designers—such as Alyce Drenth's Toronto-based Creative Avenues—has trained the H2O2 team to consider desired capacity and expandability before drafting or building. From insulation, temperature control, racking, and inventory management, the team thinks of everything, making the process painless for its clientele.

Top: Angled display shelves with LED lights and marble tabletops create visually appealing displays, while custom-lit arches frame treasured bottles.
Photograph by Steven Elphick

Bottom: Without breaking the bank, entry-level racking, horizontal display shelves, stem racks, beautiful tabletops, and LED lights come together to make a gorgeous cellar.
Photograph by H2O2 Wine Cellar Design

Facing Page: A grand entry worthy of the fine wine beyond its glass and cherry wood doors greets all who enter.
Photograph by Steven Elphick

Specially trained in proper cellar building requirements, the team is readily equipped for framing, insulation, drywalling, and installing vapor barriers and flooring. These techniques provide model storage conditions ranging from ideal room temperature and perfect levels of humidity to primo ventilation, adequate darkness, non-aromatic wooden racks, preferred bottle placement, and moisture-free floors. Their work is known for exceptional detail, ensuring each cellar will last a lifetime—or possibly two.

A perfect combination of science and art, the cellars are meant to deter mold and bacteria from penetrating the wine through its cork—which could compromise its flavor and integrity—and also prevent the breakdown of precious tannins, all the while displaying a proud collection of vintages. Patrons are able to manage cellars online, thanks to a cellar management program with optional cataloging and collection bar-coding.

Right: A 3 ½-by-4 ½-foot-wide closet was converted into an attractive wine cellar adjacent to the dining room.
Photograph by Deanna Rooke

Facing Page Top: Custom dark-stained woods and light natural stone make an efficient wine cellar an elegant design feature to the home.
Photograph by Deanna Rooke

Facing Page Bottom Left: A floor-to-ceiling glass door provides an unobtrusive entrance to the wine cellar.
Photograph by Deanna Rooke

Facing Page Bottom Right: H2O2 Wine Cellar Design owner and avid wine collector Wilfred Yu.
Photograph by Steven Elphick

Humble Bread

Prince Edward County

Baking naturally leavened bread in a wood-fired oven yields both challenges and rewards for Humble Bread owners Henry Willis and Natalie Normand. Whether they are stacking and loading 20 cords of hardwood yearly to fuel the oven or making 400 handcrafted loaves of bread per bake, the rewards reaped while living in beautiful Prince Edward County can hardly be measured. Making nutritious bread for their community and enjoying a sustainable lifestyle on the land makes the work worthwhile.

Humble Bread was established in Scarborough, Ontario, in 2006 as a micro-business that baked sourdough bread inside of a backyard-built, wood-burning oven at home. Five years later, a gut-reaction purchase of a farm in Prince Edward County brought with it a 140-year-old post-and-beam heritage barn that required renovation. Its classic gambrel roof, which is a typical feature of local barns, and original structure were preserved by the couple during its transformation into a bakeshop. Furthering the shop's historical sentiment, a demolished church in Picton provided the oven's red brick façade.

Humble, meaning modest, refers to the bread's simple ingredients of grain, water, and salt. The area is rich with farming history, which is reflected in the natural and locally sourced ingredients in the bakery's breads. Humble Bread's fields offer rich soil with which to grow grains and other crops. The farm also contains a mature vineyard—an unexpected surprise—with five grape varietals outsourced to local wineries.

Top: Humble Bread is housed in a heritage barn.

Middle: A beautiful wheat stock was skillfully incorporated into the façade of the oven; the image pays homage to the fundamental element of bread.

Bottom: A county sourdough loaf bakes on the 6-by-10-foot masonry hearth.

Facing Page: A variety of seeded sourdough loaves are ready for market.
Photographs by Steven Elphick

Natalie—senior vice president of wheat—and Henry— chief baking officer—are the humble hands behind the all-natural leavened bread, which contains no commercial yeast or artificial ingredients. Made primarily from local and estate-grown ingredients, loaves such as County Sourdough, Whole Wheat Multigrain, Sunflower Spelt, Prince Edward Miche, Cider Raisin Grain, and Buckwheat Fife are popular choices available year-round, while seasonal breads can also be found.

Dedicated to promoting the many nutritional benefits of naturally leavened breads, Humble Bread uses a fermented mix of water and flour inhabited by wild yeasts that thrive on the surface of all grains, fruits, vegetables, and are even in the air and soil. Preserving the naturally occurring good bacteria converts simple sugars into lactic and acetic acid, which organically leavens and flavors the dough. Health benefits derived from this process range from lowered insulin responses to improved glucose tolerance, a stimulated immune system, and allowance for better mineral absorption. The nature-approved approach makes a good argument for the beneficial properties of Humble Bread's loaves.

Top: Henry, Natalie, and Miche.

Bottom: Bread is unloaded from the oven using a wooden peel.

Facing Page: Handcrafted, naturally leavened methods yield one-of-a-kind loaves.
Photographs by Steven Elphick

NOTL Wine Jewelry

Niagara-on-the-Lake

Artists draw inspiration from the world around them, so it only makes sense that Thuy Nguyen of NOTL Wine Jewelry draws her inspiration from the picturesque Ontario wine country that is located not far from her home studio. Surrounded by manicured vineyards and beautiful wineries producing some of the world's finest vintages, Thuy felt the spark of creativity and the concept for NOTL—which stands for Niagara-on-the-Lake—Wine Jewelry was born. Since 1992, Thuy has created one-of-a-kind, private label designs for stylish wine lovers all over the world. Her jewelry creations, which range from statement necklaces made from semi-precious gems to delicate, Swarovski crystal-embellished earrings, continue to garner respect from the Ontario wineries and private customers alike.

Jewelry design has long been a passion of Thuy's. With her background in fashion and design guiding her daily observations, Thuy was immediately impressed by the look of the manicured vineyards that stretch across the slopes of Ontario in spring. The minimalist feel of the natural world created a dichotomy that was too striking for Thuy to ignore, and she and her husband, Hank, moved to the area in 2000.

NOTL Wine Jewelry offers an array of designs for the discerning jewelry collector; its wearable works of art run the gamut from modern designs to vintage themes, all under collection names associated with the vineyards of Canadian wine country. Just as respected winemakers choose natural ingredients of high quality, so does Thuy.

Top: The Code Rosé necklace and earrings celebrate the month of October and pay homage to the pinkest of wines.

Bottom: Like sun-kissed chardonnay, golden Swarovski crystals shine on the Chardonnay Cool Climate necklace.

Facing Page: Rich merlot inspires some of the red wine collections.
Photographs by Steven Elphick

NOTL Wine Jewelry is crafted with Swarovski crystals, select gemstones, and precious metals, rather than glass replicas and lesser metals. The original designs are sold at local wineries and, in turn, NOTL Wine Jewelry participates in the locations' various annual events and fundraisers.

Like the wine vintages from which she gains creative vision, Thuy's designs are only available in limited quantities with some remaining strictly one-of-a-kind. The pieces of wearable wine jewelry reflect the region: "grapevines" of gems curl from sterling silver necklaces, merlot-colored crystals cascade like red wine drops from the wearer's neck, and other designs with varietal names—riesling, chardonnay, and rosé—illustrate just how much the Ontario wine culture has influenced Thuy's work.

Above Left: The colder months demand darker colors, such as the Black Grapes necklace, which drips from the neck of the wearer.

Above Right: Icewine, a specialty of many local wineries, is the inspiration for the ice crystal and jet Swarovski crystal necklace.

Left: NOTL Wine Jewelry artist Thuy Nguyen with her husband and partner, Hank Hofer.

Facing Page: Pearls drip down one's neck in the White Grapes design, bringing to mind the fruit of Ontario wine regions.
Photographs by Steven Elphick

Rosehill Wine Cellars

Toronto

Just as a great wine is the culmination of a long series of steps governed by talent, tradition, and expertise, so too is a great wine cellar. A masterfully constructed wine cellar combines the right materials and cooling equipment with expert design, fabrication, and installation.

Under the Rosehill Wine Cellars banner, owner Gary LaRose leads a construction firm that designs and builds custom cellars in private homes, clubs, and restaurants. The construction operations are supported by Rosehill's dedicated state-of-the-art wine rack manufacturing facility, and a retail store and showroom that offers wine service items and accessories.

In the mid-'90s Gary was involved in high-end interior renovations and was engaged to do some work for *Wine Access* editor David Lawrason. During the course of the home renovation, David introduced Gary to the joys of tasting and the curatorial aspects of building a collection. Gary soon found himself enrolled in one of David's wine courses. This course was a turning point in Gary's life, and he fell in love with the kinship, the discussions, and the experience of enjoying wine with likeminded aficionados. This new appreciation led to an epiphany to combine his passion for building and his new-found passion for wine. From this combination Rosehill Wine Cellars was born, and a new direction in design and construction of custom wine cellars began. Gary now firmly believes that you can only build great wine cellars if you have extensive construction knowledge and an understanding of the sensitivities of wine storage.

Top: A focal point is created by the use of a barrel ceiling and open niche on the back wall. All Heart Redwood racking has interesting details with pilasters and trim. A black granite counter and multicolor floor slate adds to the warmth of the room.

Bottom: The angle display in the natural walnut racking is a great way to view labels while keeping the cork wet.

Facing Page: The famous tower of walnut wine racking inside the Aria Ristorante in downtown Toronto stretches 23 feet high and is functional as well as a showcase for the restaurant's impressive collection.
Photographs courtesy of Rosehill Wine Cellars

Gary runs the construction arm of the business, a venture robust enough to require three full-time crews, while his wife Sue helms the retail side of the operation, shipping wine storage, serveware, and accessories around the world. Their subsidiary, Rosehill Wine Racks, is a dedicated 15,000-square-foot factory where computer-aided manufacturing brings dream cellar scenarios to life. High-tech, precision manufacturing using German and Italian machinery transforms raw materials into installation-ready components for custom cellars. For the tradesperson or do-it-yourself builder, Rosehill also produces Premier Cru Kit Racks, prefab components that can be shipped quickly, are easy to install, and offer the very best in quality. Rosehill supports its hands-on customers with construction tips and an online layout guide to shepherd them through the process of configuring and installing racking systems.

In addition to industry standard redwood, Rosehill offers a choice of racking materials including sapele, walnut, white oak, maple, Douglas fir, and cherry.

As old and storied as wine appreciation may be, its gadgetry continues to evolve. Rosehill's retail website and showroom offer an unparalleled collection of glassware, handcrafted sommelier glasses, furniture constructed from reclaimed wine barrels, decanters,

Above: Walnut millwork along with the vaulted ceiling covered in slice bricks provides a unique and Old World look that is warm and inviting.

Right: Walnut racking with a tasting table with an onyx top and lighting from underneath shows the creative fun that can be had with cellar design and materials.

Facing Page: A famous Canadian rock star commissioned a contemporary design of dark-stained maple to elegantly store a variety of bottle types.
Photographs courtesy of Rosehill Wine Cellars

and a host of maps of the world's top grape-producing areas. One of the greatest assets of Rosehill is the knowledge and expertise that the long-term staff has accumulated over the years. They are able to assist customers with any topic: wine cellars, racking, cooling units, wine cabinets, accessories, and more. In this business, knowledge grows only from years of experience with many diversified wine storage situations. Whether customers drop into the showroom to browse and chat or surf the website, Rosehill's years of hands-on experience ensure that customers will always find solutions to their storage and accessory needs.

Complementing Rosehill's expertise in building custom cellars for private clients—ranging from bank CEOs and mining company executives to rock musicians and NHL players—its commercial installations include the 2011 ARIDO award-winning Aria Ristorante, Platinum Lounge at the Air Canada Center, Eleven, Far Niente, Canoe, Soto Soto, The National Club, The Albany Club, Casino Niagara, and several wineries in the Niagara Peninsula.

With expertise developed through their passion and experience in building extraordinary wine cellars since 1995, the Rosehill team has every stage of wine storage and service covered.

Left: In a custom-built walnut wine cabinet in a Yorkville condo, bottles are displayed in a horizontal position on metal frames so that the labels can be viewed. A water cool ducted unit controls temperature throughout the cabinet.

Facing Page: A variety of racks, all done in natural sapele, allows for an interesting mix of storage options consisting of angle displays, 12-bottle bins, solid diamond bins, and an arch with a niche on the back elevation. A barrel ceiling was created to take advantage of the 10-foot ceiling height.
Photographs courtesy of Rosehill Wine Cellars

Upper Canada Cheese Company

Jordan Station

Wayne Philbrick, founding owner of Upper Canada Cheese Company, grew up on a peach farm and has been enthusiastic about local produce ever since. His enthusiasm for the benefits of rural living expanded during a trip to Quebec, where he became enthralled with cheese and its appetizing properties, especially when paired with balancing wine. Seeking out an avenue for his newfound interest, Wayne began to experiment with cheese in his spare time. His hobby naturally matured into a delicate art, and the first small-but-modern creamery constructed in Niagara in generations soon followed.

Making artisan cheese the pure and simple way, Upper Canada Cheese derives milk from the Comfort Family Farm, which has been a Saint Anne's fixture for five generations and counting. Nurturing pasture-fed Guernsey cows, the farm's organic milk is both animal-friendly and of superior quality. Because the cows are well cared for, the creamery can confidently transform the delectable milk into cheeses exhibiting uncommon taste and texture due to a subtle range of flavors that are influenced by many factors including seasons and feed. Located only minutes away from the creamery, the purest Guernsey milk is delivered first thing every morning, ensuring freshness.

The creamery's signature cheese is Niagara Gold, one of the most sought-after cheeses in Ontario. The orange rind-wrapped wheel matures for four months in a temperature- and humidity-controlled cellar, its rich flavor revealing earthy undertones, reminiscent of

Top: Camelot is a reserve champion aged goat cheese.

Middle: Comfort Cream is ready for tasting at the creamery's gourmet boutique.

Bottom: Upper Canada Cheese uses only pure Guernsey milk from animals pastured on the Niagara Peninsula.

Facing Page: Comfort Cream, a bloomy Camembert, and the famous Niagara Gold are all handcrafted from pure Guernsey milk.
Photographs by Steven Elphick

the Niagara terroir's clay and silt nuances—just one benefit of grass-fed cows. Comfort Cream is another dairy delight, its bloomy rind concealing 300 grams of round Camembert goodness. The locally made artisan cheeses are in great demand from neighboring wineries as they exquisitely complement wines whose grapes grew from the same soil. Upper Canada Cheese Company's acclaim has reached as far south as Texas and even across the pond into Europe. Although the operation is small, and intends to remain so, its reputation for quality is large and growing.

A visit to the Jordan Station creamery and gourmet boutique promises a tantalizing exploration. Tutorials of how fine cheese is made are almost as interesting as the endless amount of aged artisan samples that taunt the lactose intolerant. An assortment of gourmet sauces, preserves, fresh jams, oils, and dressings—many of which are also produced in Niagara—are all part of a constantly evolving selection of goods.

Left: The creamery in Jordan Station, architecturally designed for latter-day railway stations. The design is an homage to the milk trains that would bring the milk every morning to the creameries and drop the cans railside.

Facing Page Top Right: Founding partner Wayne Philbrick.

Facing Page Top Left: The gourmet boutique is filled with local products.

Facing Page Bottom: One of the finely controlled ripening rooms.
Photographs by Steven Elphick

The Waring House

Picton

There is something special about stepping into a centuries-old house in the heart of Ontario wine country and being surrounded by reminders of the province's proud rural heritage. From rooms furnished with antiques to meals crafted with local farm produce, The Waring House is a place where Old World charm meets modern sensibilities.

The central structure of The Waring House is a stone farmhouse that has stood at Waring's Corners in Prince Edward County since the 1820s. In 1995, Chris and Norah Rogers purchased the property. Since that time, The Waring House has expanded to include 49 guestrooms, a restaurant and a pub, a recreational cooking school, a spa, meeting facilities, and an artist-in-residence. The grounds boast extensive gardens, charming window boxes, herb and vegetable gardens, and a vineyard.

Chris and Norah have made it their goal to provide an atmosphere of warm, rural hospitality and a sense of history. Furnished with Canadian antiques and art, the inn rooms are individually decorated, making a stay feel more like lodging in the home of a family member rather than in a commercial inn.

The Rogers are also passionate about environmental sustainability. In the two lodges built in 2008, solar-powered hot water systems and geothermal heating and air conditioning are standard. Raised in rural Ontario, Norah has had a lifelong commitment to quality food that is locally sourced and lovingly prepared—a concept at the heart of what is now known as the Slow Food movement. In addition to the onsite kitchen garden, many of the ingredients used in the pub and restaurant are sourced from local farms and meat and cheese producers.

Top: A statue of St. Francis graces the back garden, a popular spot for wedding photographs.

Middle: Amelia's Garden Restaurant features the finest in food, much of it sourced from local producers.

Bottom: Owners Chris and Norah Rogers, with Katie and Annie.

Facing Page: The stone farmhouse, built in the 1860s, is at the heart of The Waring House property and houses The Barley Room Pub, Amelia's Garden Restaurant, and several guestrooms.
Photographs by Steven Elphick

Members of the culinary staff share the joy of cooking with guests who enroll in classes at the onsite cookery school. The school runs private group classes that serve as team-building exercises for those utilizing the inn's meeting space for corporate events, while the school's regular open classes attract individual vacationers and locals alike. The Garden Spa, also located at The Waring House, offers a variety of spa services for individuals, couples, and groups, such as bridal parties.

The Rogers' attraction to historical architecture led them in 2001 to purchase Claramount, a colonial revival mansion in a park-like setting on Picton Bay. After years of restoration, using the original architect's drawings, the mansion is now home to an inn, a fine dining restaurant, and a spa, offering a full range of esthetic and therapeutic services and specializing in Kneipp and Vichy water treatments.

The couple are also the proud owners of Barley Days Brewery, a craft brewery in Picton that produces a number of year-round and seasonal beers using such local ingredients as hops, cherries, and maple syrup. A retail location in Picton, Waring House Gourmet also gives the Rogers a chance to sell food and gift products for Prince Edward County food producers and artisans.

Top: The Prince Edward Room in the main house is used as a dining room and meeting room.

Middle: Alec Lunn and Mark Despault, better known as The Frère Brothers, are one of the many local live music acts featured in The Barley Room Pub.

Bottom: The interior of the Vineyard View Cottage.

Facing Page Top: Claramount Inn & Spa is a colonial revival mansion on Picton Bay.

Facing Page Top Left: Suites at Claramount Inn & Spa are individually decorated.

Facing Page Bottom Left: The Spa at Claramount specializes in Vichy and Kneipp water treatments.

Facing Page Bottom Right: Clara's Restaurant, at Claramount, features the best in seasonal and regional food.
Photographs by Steven Elphick

Wine Awakenings

Niagara-on-the-Lake

S pawned in Niagara-on-the-Lake, in the heart of Canada's major wine-producing region and chief manufacturer of the world's greatest icewines, a privately owned company takes pride in being a small but committed group of wine professionals dedicated to enhancing the enjoyment of wine. With only a handful of closely knit collaborators, the company has diligently worked toward a new take on wine education by utilizing the most advanced industry techniques and promoting leisure education-turned-lifelong skill.

Approximately 10 years ago, the method was devised by Gary Pickering, a professor of biological sciences and psychology and a world-renowned researcher. While the concept of a wine aroma kit is not new, a new vision and application for the idea followed, thanks to the rebranding, redevelopment, and remarketing of the kits by its present ownership. When liberated and enlightened, awakened senses tend to appreciate wine's well-kept secrets, promising a sensorial journey that will leave participants seeking further discovery.

Wine aroma kits were developed to educate, train, and entertain. Students in the wine and culinary arts, hospitality professionals, sommeliers, connoisseurs, and instructors use these kits to increase their ability to correctly decipher aromas found in wine. Wine Awakenings aroma kits are produced to correspond with specific wine varietals, making its product unique and favored among wine enthusiasts, hobbyists, and anyone who wishes to enhance their knowledge of wines.

Top and Middle: Naming what we smell is no easy task.

Bottom: The series includes: cabernet sauvignon, chardonnay, pinot noir, red wine, white wine, wine faults, and the newest, white icewine.

Facing Page: Each kit is a collection of the 12 most common aromas found in each popular varietal, along with beautifully illustrated descriptive literature to guide the sensory experience.
Photographs by Steven Elphick

Appreciating wine to its fullest can be greatly rewarding. Like any art, education and proper tools are a necessity when applying a new practice or mastering an old one. Once reserved for culinary professionals, wine aroma kits are tools that teach users to detect trace influences in wine, just as critics do. The demystification of wines for everyday consumers is a highly regarded goal, achieved by producing a series of varietal-specific wine aroma kits that assist consumers in identifying scents that would normally go undetected. Comprised of tools that were once considered industry exclusives, wine aroma kits now include the world's first and only icewine kit, one of seven available through Wine Awakenings. Each artfully crafted kit contains 12 vials, a descriptive scent card for each aroma, and a personal taste profile with an online interactive guide. The company's website is also designed to support a sensory experience and offers many exclusive tasting tips and other relevant information.

Matchless and customizable, the kits make unforgettable mementos that are engaging, entertaining, and educational. Welcoming users to experience the harmonious elements of science and art in wine, the kits ignite imagination and discovery, from first sniff to discerning lips.

Top: *Wine Expert in a Box* is a self-paced certification program that contains patented technology and proven distance learning tools to bring students the experience and expertise of wine hospitality.

Bottom: The core team at Wine Awakenings includes Rita, Amato, and Maria.

Facing Page: Expanding your repertoire of aromas is an intriguing experience, especially when the focus is on wine.
Photographs by Steven Elphick

The Wine Establishment

Toronto

Experts believe that wine is a living liquid, created by the combination of wild yeast and fermenting grapes, that continues to develop even after it has been bottled, corked, and shelved away. Like many living things, wine can be influenced by its environments. For example, fluctuating temperatures, uncontrolled humidity, and exposure to light can compromise its very structure by altering defining characteristics such as aromas, tannins, and flavors. Because a vintage wine can transform into a vinegar-like substance due to improper care, wine enthusiasts should follow certain guidelines when putting a vintage to bed, thereby ensuring that the wine will be at its peak for a later celebration.

Finding and identifying a beloved vintage after years of tastings and errors is the first step to an adored collection of hand-selected vintages. The second, and debatably the most important step, is preserving the bottle for a special occasion, one that will herald memories of the day it was discovered, where it was found, and why it was chosen. While the concept of cellaring is not a new one, cutting-edge walk-in designs of exceptional craftsmanship, along with an extensive selection of free-standing options, offer wines a necessary repose from character-altering vibration, bright light, and odors, in addition to being temperature and humidity controlled.

Specializing in luxury commercial and residential wine cellars, The Wine Establishment is dedicated to properly prolonging the life of wine through state-of-the-art storage. Its stellar cellars have graced the pages of *House and Home* and *Canadian Living*, reinforcing its

Top: The Wine Establishment's showroom is located in beautiful Berkeley Castle, originally a knitting factory dating from the mid-19th century and located in the heart of old Toronto.

Bottom: Innovatively designed display shelves inside a door frame highlight a special collection of classic wines.

Facing Page: The Wine Cellar Design Centre at The Wine Establishment's Toronto showroom is an inspiring location for visitors to consider cellar projects.
Photographs by Steven Elphick

leadership role in the industry and a well-earned reputation. Led by architect Greg Ziesmann, the firm approaches each project from a building-science perspective, employing the know-how of mechanical engineers, designers, and finish carpenters from conception to construction to completion. Large projects, such as 10,000-plus bottle turn-key cellars are found in both residences—like a Toronto home with galvanized metal racking and a 15,000-bottle cellar and reserve room—and businesses such as the Calgary Petroleum Club, which benefits from a 14,000-bottle boardroom backdrop in all-heart mahogany racking. As wine cellars move out of the basement, more intimate and attractive cellars are being constructed as an integral part of the entertaining space of the home.

The Wine Establishment offers only the finest free-standing cellaring options for homeowners, such as Liebherr and EuroCave, as well as quality Canadian-made wine cellars from Cavavin and Les Celliers Rosyma. As North America's leading supplier and designer of racking and climate-controlled cellaring systems, the firm has been an industry leader for more than 25 years. At the University of British Columbia's prestigious School of Viticulture it was commissioned to create a dazzling wine cellar library that accommodates up to 22,000 bottles for research purposes. The custom climate control system constantly monitors air

Top: Galley-style storage allows for easy access to all of a collector's fine vintages.
Photograph by Steven Elphick

Bottom: Racking aisles run off a central hub, making the best use of an unusually shaped space in a 2,000-bottle cellar.
Photograph by Steven Elphick

Facing Page Top: Classic antique finishes, custom lighting, and unique furnishings bring a lovely mood to the 6,000-bottle wine cellar.
Photograph by James J. Burry

Facing Page Bottom: A separate tasting room outside the doors to the cellar allows the homeowners to entertain in comfort while still being surrounded by a wonderful wine atmosphere.
Photograph by James J. Burry

flow and quality while precise lighting ensures vintages are kept in prime condition. Its work with the hospitality industry can also be seen commercially in fine-dining establishments such as Harbour Sixty Steakhouse, whose chrome-plated metal racking system effectively and beautifully merchandises the restaurant's impressive wine selection.

Additional services, from wine cabinet installations to freestanding coolers, are perfect for space-saving wine aficionados or beginning collectors who dwell within an impermanent situation. The Wine Establishment's downtown Toronto showroom offers visitors eye-catching displays of expert-chosen stemware, corkscrews, decanters, aerators, funnels, and aroma kits. The handsome environment is perfectly suited for corporate functions and private soirées hosted by hospitality experts. An extensive assortment of modern accessories including international brands like Riedel Crystal, Spiegelau, Forge de Laguiole, and Le Nez du Vin are ideal for gifting or corporate incentive baskets, while fine cookware by Le Creuset is also available for ambitious wine and fare endeavors.

Right: Flooring featuring corks from the owners' collection commemorates treasured bottles. Zero-heat lighting from below provides a dramatic flourish to the design.

Facing Page Top: The 800-bottle crystal wine cube integrates seamlessly with the kitchen, immediately engaging the eye.

Facing Page Bottom Left: A noiseless custom climate control system means that the wine cellar never gets in the way of great conversation in the elegant entertainment space.

Facing Page Bottom Right: Enomatic's service and preservation system allows four bottles to be opened for by-the-glass service over several weeks without sacrificing quality. The inventory management terminal tracks bottles on their way in and out of the cellar.
Photographs by Steven Elphick

INDEX

SPECTACULAR WINERIES

ONTARIO TEAM

ASSOCIATE PUBLISHER: Patricia Butler

ART DIRECTOR: Emily A. Kattan

GRAPHIC DESIGNER: Lilian Oliveira

EDITOR: Megan Winkler

MANAGING PRODUCTION COORDINATOR: Kristy Randall

HEADQUARTERS TEAM

PUBLISHER: Brian G. Carabet

PUBLISHER: John A. Shand

GRAPHIC DESIGNER: Jen Ray

GRAPHIC DESIGNER: Lauren Schneider

MANAGING EDITOR: Lindsey Wilson

SENIOR EDITOR: Sarah Tangney

EDITOR: Alicia Berger

EDITOR: Jennifer Nelson

EDITOR: Nicole Pearce

EDITOR: Sarah Reiss

TRAFFIC SUPERVISOR: Drea Williams

DEVELOPMENT & DISTRIBUTION SPECIALIST: Rosalie Z. Wilson

ADMINISTRATIVE COORDINATOR: Amanda Mathers

ADMINISTRATIVE ASSISTANT: Aubrey Grunewald

PANACHE PARTNERS, LLC
1424 Gables Court
Plano, TX 75075
469.246.6060
www.panache.com

Karlo Estates, page 228
Painting by Sherry Martin
Photograph by Steven Elphick

THE PANACHE COLLECTION

Dream Homes Series
An Exclusive Showcase of the
Finest Architects, Designers and Builders

Carolinas	New Jersey
Chicago	Northern California
Coastal California	Ohio & Pennsylvania
Colorado	Pacific Northwest
Deserts	Philadelphia
Florida	South Florida
Georgia	Southwest
Los Angeles	Tennessee
Metro New York	Texas
Michigan	Washington, D.C.
Minnesota	
New England	

Spectacular Homes Series
An Exclusive Showcase of the Finest Interior Designers

California	Metro New York
Carolinas	Ohio & Pennsylvania
Chicago	Pacific Northwest
Colorado	Philadelphia
Florida	South Florida
Georgia	Southwest
Heartland	Tennessee
London	Texas
Michigan	Toronto
Minnesota	Washington, D.C.
New England	Western Canada

Perspectives on Design Series
Design Philosophies Expressed
by Leading Professionals

California	Minnesota
Carolinas	New England
Chicago	New York
Colorado	Pacific Northwest
Florida	South Florida
Georgia	Southwest
Great Lakes	Toronto
London	Western Canada

Art of Celebration Series
Inspiration and Ideas from
Top Event Professionals

Chicago & the Greater Midwest
Colorado
Georgia
New England
New York
Northern California
South Florida
Southern California
Southern Style
Southwest
Toronto
Washington, D.C.

City by Design Series
An Architectural Perspective

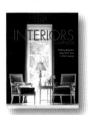

Atlanta
Charlotte
Chicago
Dallas
Denver
New York
Orlando
Phoenix
San Francisco
Texas

Spectacular Wineries Series
A Captivating Tour of Established,
Estate and Boutique Wineries

California's Central Coast
Napa Valley
New York
Ontario
Sonoma County
Texas
Washington

Experience Series
The Most Interesting Attractions,
Hotels, Restaurants, and Shops

Austin & the Hill Country
Boston
British Columbia
Chicago
Southern California
Twin Cities

Interiors Series
Leading Designers Reveal Their Most Brilliant Spaces

Florida
Midwest
New York
Southeast
Washington, D.C.

Spectacular Golf Series
The Most Scenic and Challenging Golf Holes

Arizona
Colorado
Ontario
Pacific Northwest
Southeast
Texas
Western Canada

Weddings Series
Captivating Destinations and Exceptional Resources
Introduced by the Finest Event Planners

Southern California

Specialty Titles
The Finest in Unique Luxury Lifestyle Publications

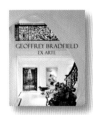

21st Century Homes
Cloth and Culture: Couture Creations of Ruth E. Funk
Distinguished Inns of North America
Dolls Etcetera
Extraordinary Homes California
Geoffrey Bradfield Ex Arte
Into the Earth: A Wine Cave Renaissance
Luxurious Interiors
Napa Valley Iconic Wineries
Shades of Green Tennessee
Spectacular Hotels
Spectacular Restaurants of Texas
Visions of Design

Panache Books App
Inspiration at Your Fingertips

Download the Panache
Books app in the iTunes
Store to access select
Panache Partners
publications. Each book
offers inspiration at your
fingertips.

Panache Partners, LLC   1424 Gables Court   Plano, Texas 75075   469.246.6060   www.panache.com